"...know firsthand that Gabriele and Debi live the delicious life of 'Super Tuscans.' This cookbook is about passion, family, and the most satisfying Italian recipes."

—Bobby Flay

"A deliciously simple yet sophisticated collection of Italian comfort that embraces you immediately, mirroring everything I love about Debi and Gabriele themselves!"

—Lee Schrager, founder of the South Beach and New York City Wine & Food Festivals

"Gabriele and Debi bring the taste of Tuscany right into your own kitchen, welcoming you to their table, so you feel like a member of their family. *Super Tuscan* brings those flavors home with unfussy Italian techniques and fresh ingredients. A glorious celebration of Tuscany!"

—David Lebovitz, author of *L'Appart* and *My Paris Kitchen*

"Gabriele and Debi cook the most delicious food with love and joy. Their generosity, knowledge, and passion come through in every recipe! Full of flavor and a contemporary flair deeply rooted in Italian family tradition!"

—Zac Posen

"This book represents everything great food is all about. Food is about passion, commitments, risk, love, trust, and laughter. Gabriele and Debi are all about that, and they're pretty bad-ass cooks as well. Best of all, they live a real life with their two beautiful girls, which makes this book a one-of-a-kind experience for the home cook looking for Italian inspiration."

—Andrew Zimmern

"Yum-yum! Super Tuscan-y!! Mmmmmm!!!"

—Paul "Pee-wee Herman" Reubens

SUPER TUSCAN

HERITAGE RECIPES
AND SIMPLE PLEASURES
FROM OUR KITCHEN
TO YOUR TABLE

GABRIELE CORCOS

and

DEBI MAZAR

with

RICK RODGERS

TOUCHSTONE
New York   London   Toronto   Sydney   New Delhi

Touchstone
An Imprint of Simon & Schuster, Inc.
1230 Avenue of the Americas
New York, NY 10020

First Touchstone hardcover edition October 2017

TOUCHSTONE and colophon are registered trademarks of Simon & Schuster, Inc.

For information about special discounts for bulk purchases,
please contact Simon & Schuster Special Sales at 1-866-506-1949
or business@simonandschuster.com.

The Simon & Schuster Speakers Bureau can bring authors to your live event.
For more information or to book an event contact the Simon & Schuster Speakers Bureau
at 1-866-248-3049 or visit our website at www.simonspeakers.com.

Design by Erich Hobbing
All photos by Eric Wolfinger

Manufactured in the United States of America

1   3   5   7   9   10   8   6   4   2

Library of Congress Cataloging-in-Publication Data

Names: Corcos, Gabriele, author. | Mazar, Debi, author. | Rodgers, Rick
Title: Super Tuscan : heritage recipes and simple pleasures from our kitchen to your table/
by Gabriele Corcos and Debi Mazar ; with Rick Rodgers.
Description: New York : Touchstone, 2017. | Description based on print version record and
CIP data provided by publisher; resource not viewed.
Identifiers: LCCN 2017007208 (print) | LCCN 2017028605 (ebook)
Subjects: LCSH: Cooking, Italian—Tuscan style. | Cooking, American. | BISAC: COOKING / Regional & Ethnic /
Mediterranean. | COOKING / Entertaining. | LCGFT: Cookbooks.
Classification: LCC TX723.2.T86 (ebook) | LCC TX723.2.T86 C686 2017 (print) |DDC 641.5945—dc23
LC record available at https://lccn.loc.gov/2017007208

ISBN 978-1-5011-4359-5
ISBN 978-1-5011-4361-8 (ebook)

To the ones that grow and harvest
To the ones that hunt and fish
To the ones that cook and feed
To the ones that eat and celebrate

CONTENTS

VEGETABLES AND GRAINS

DESSERTS

INTRODUCTION

Anyone who has seen us cooking together knows that we have a couple of concurrent love affairs running. The first passionate relationship we are speaking of is with each other, and by extension, with our family. And our other serious romance is with Tuscany, the incredibly beautiful region in Italy where Gabriele was born and where we first met in a love-at-first-sight experience right out of the movies. (Our first date was in the Piazza Santo Spirito in Florence, a tough act to follow.) Crusty, unsalted bread; verdant green extra-virgin olive oil; elegant and forthright Chianti; pasta sauce made with wild boar; the poetry of Dante and the art of Michelangelo . . . if it is Tuscan, we love it.

GABRIELE: I was raised on a farm in Fiesole, in the hills overlooking Florence where practically every piece of real estate comes with its own stand of olive trees and a vineyard. To a Tuscan, making your own oil and wine is not just a romantic notion, it is a way of life. Cooking and eating with the seasons, heirloom recipes, careful sourcing of food (as well as growing or raising your own), and attention to healthful eating are not new notions to a Tuscan. Nine times out of ten, a Tuscan knows exactly where his or her food comes from, including where the mushrooms were foraged or the name of the chicken that laid the eggs. Once you grow up on a farm, it is difficult to shake off the knowledge of how food gets on your plate.

Debi has lived all over New York, and we've lived together in Los Angeles. We now make our life in a little corner of Brooklyn called Windsor Terrace. It is a diverse, thriving community tucked between the southern edge of Park Slope and the famous Green-Wood Cemetery, final resting place of many well-known New Yorkers.

DEBI: We returned to New York so our daughters, Evelina and Giulia, can see where Mom (that's me) came from and to give them the experience of living in a city that personifies "urban living" with all its challenges and perks. We have come to realize that no matter where we settle, we always bring the Tuscan way of life, its traditions, and its cooking into our day-to-day existence as much as possible. We may not have olive trees in the backyard, but we cook and eat in the Tuscan manner. Whether we have a picnic under a maple in Prospect Park or an oak in Italy, it is still a tree and we are still dining together. And we basically make the same meal in both countries!

GABRIELE: But what is "super Tuscan," anyway? A couple of decades ago, Tuscan winemakers adopted the term "super Tuscan" to describe a new kind of wine. Chianti was, and is, made according to very strict rules within clearly defined geographical boundaries and with specific grapes, especially the classic Sangiovese. Some winemakers were making wonderful wine in neighboring regions with different, but equally good, grape varieties (Cabernet Sauvi-

gnon and merlot are examples). Some wineries began mixing Sangiovese with these grapes, and creating great wines, but they didn't conform to the time-honored Chianti standards. So, the term "super Tuscan" was born—excellent wine with Chianti's soul, although of mixed heritage.

DEBI: It occurred to us that we cook in a super-Tuscan style too. Gabriele's development as an Italian cook really took off when we lived in Los Angeles. He developed basic cooking skills growing up, helping his mom in the kitchen, acting as sous chef and server at her dinner parties to make some extra cash. These skills really came into play as a stay-at-home dad, making meals for the entire family while I was working in front of the camera. Drawing on his trove of family recipes, he developed his own style of cooking, which was mostly Italian with a slight Californian accent. For example, he embraced Mexican cooking, which, like Italian, has many herbal and spicy flavors and doesn't rely on butter.

GABRIELE: Debi showed me the local farmer's markets, and I quickly became a fan. In Italy, local outdoor markets sell household goods as well as apples, so the focus on produce and the array available was dizzying and inspiring. She also exposed me to many of the dishes she learned during her formative years in New York—from Puerto Rican stews to fried chicken and other soul food specialties, and then on to corned beef on rye.

While remaining true to my Tuscan heritage, these American influences crept into our cooking. While I was raised on *paste e ceci* and *crocchette di patate* (garbanzo bean pasta and potato croquettes), I could not resist the charms of creamy clam chowder and fudgy chocolate brownies.

Just as many super-Tuscan wines start with Sangiovese, every dish we make is distilled through the Tuscan approach to eating that I learned on the farm and we now take with us wherever we cook:

꙰ With the exception of an occasional dried bay leaf, we always cook with fresh herbs, and have even found American sources for a beloved Tuscan standard, *nipitella* (see page 10).

꙰ Our homemade desserts are made in the Tuscan fashion, and not loaded with sugar (which cannot be said of their American counterparts). We don't make desserts at home often, but when we do, it is with the very best ingredients, and that includes choosing vanilla beans over vanilla extract for true European flavor.

꙰ Radicchio is not just a salad ingredient but is cooked as *contorni* (side dishes), among other roles. Kale is not trendy to us, as it has been an essential Tuscan food, especially in the winter, for centuries.

꙰ We cook liberally with wine because alcohol truly enhances the flavors of the other ingredients—it is a fact.

꙰ Parmigiano-Reggiano finds its way into many dishes beyond being a topping. And we also use its salty, sharp cousin cheese, Pecorino Romano.

꙰ When we make macaroni and cheese, we experiment with different Italian *formaggi*. Our current favorite, Baked Truffle Cavatappi (page 127), features truffled cheese.

꙰ A trio of pork products—guanciale, pancetta, and prosciutto—is used to season vegetables, pasta sauces, and soups.

꙰ When we make a cocktail, bitter Italian liqueurs are just as important as American spirits like vodka and bourbon, and Tuscan wines are poured more often than any other kind. We serve a lot of Italian beer and sodas too.

꙰ Debi: Gabriele bakes a loaf of (salted) bread in our oven every day or so. The recipe can be found on our website: www.thetuscangun.com. When we don't bake bread, we often make the focaccia on page 23.

꙰ We get our meats hand cut at a butcher shop that is just a couple of blocks from our house (and happens to be owned by two Italian brothers), and we can pick our produce at the local farmer's market.

Super Tuscan shares our personalized version of Italian and American favorites seen through the lens of our life together. It's how we cook every day, and we have emphasized the kind of fare we make for the two of us, Evelina, and Giulia, on busy weeknights—Chicken Saltimbocca (page 195), Baked Snapper with Spinach Filling (page 149), and Pappardelle with Asparagus and Mushrooms (page 117) are just a few of our family favorites in this book. We have not neglected "company's coming" fare, either, and offer up ideas for dinner parties, such as Roast Beef with Baby Onions (page 163), and the Pancetta-Wrapped Turkey Breast with Herbs (page 201) is perfect for a small Thanksgiving gathering. Many of the recipes come directly from Gabriele's memories of cooking on the farm—Potato Croquettes (page 217), Italian Carrot Cake (page 229), and Roast Chicken alla Contadina (page 191) are pulled from Mamma's recipe box. You'll find wine (and beer) recommendations for some recipes too. Yes, beer. Gabriele loves his beer!

We welcome you into our kitchen, and we hope that these recipes also inspire you to infuse your cooking with Tuscan traditions.

Gabriele Corcos
Debi Mazar

OUR SUPER-TUSCAN LIFE

Both of us have certain family heirloom recipes ingrained in our memories, and we recall their details every time we cook. We sometimes follow recipes from books, but most of the time we rely on our reserve of culinary knowledge, which we learned from actually cooking night after night over the years. But variations of those basic dishes of roast chicken, big bowls of pasta, and sautéed fish show up again and again on our table to feed our family and friends. Returning to our roots, both American and Tuscan, define what happens in our kitchen.

OUR KITCHEN

You have heard it said that the kitchen is the heart of the home. At our house, the kitchen is more than just where we cook and eat. It is a gathering place, too, where we come together as a family to talk, share, and laugh. Our funniest and saddest conversations still take place around our kitchen table.

Our kitchen is admittedly larger than others in New York, but then again, New York is infamous for its small kitchens. It is also much smaller than the one we had in Los Angeles, so we have learned how to organize the room for maximum efficiency.

Minimize drawers: It is a drag to rummage around a crowded "junk drawer" to find that single spoon. We are very organized because we just don't have the time to waste. Utensils are kept outside of drawers for easy, visible access. We have a large canister to hold our collection of spoons, a lineup of various knives on the counter ready to be pulled into action, and a metal grid for hanging ladles and the like. Being able to grab a spoon at a moment's notice saves a lot of time.

Have a working table: Our marble-topped table is the centerpiece of our kitchen. Debi had it specially made from a marble remnant in the Bronx and repurposed two restaurant table bases for a bargain-basement treasure. We eat on it, sure, but we also work on it. Its smooth, cool top is perfect for kneading bread and rolling out crostata dough. If it were made of wood, it wouldn't be half as useful.

Stock up on the cutting boards: If we want to cut something on our marble table, we use a cutting board. Have a few cutting boards so you can share prep chores with friends and family. We like plastic boards for prepping ingredients because they are so easy to clean—just wash in hot soapy water or pop them into the dishwasher. But we use our wooden boards for slicing bread and as rustic-looking serving platters too. It is especially useful to have a carving board with a grooved well running around its perimeter to catch the carving juices from chicken and roasts.

1

Bowls are your best friends: When we are cooking, we bring out a stack of nested bowls for easy access. We prefer light and sturdy stainless steel bowls. Our bowls get a lot of use and we only use our ceramic or pottery bowls for serving.

Keep your appliances handy: We all struggle with having enough counter space. But if you have easy access to your most necessary appliances, you will cook more efficiently. A list of favorite appliances changes from person to person, but ours include an immersion blender (perfect for blending canned tomatoes into puree), and a stand mixer (for freeing up your hands when making cookie dough and cake batter).

With skillets, think big: We are a family of four, so we want to cook four servings of food at a time: a cut-up chicken, four pork chops, four fish fillets . . . The average skillet just isn't large enough to hold that much food comfortably. Also, if the food is crowded, it won't brown well. Invest in a very large nonstick skillet, 12 to 14 inches in diameter. We use our skillet every day. Some cooks feel that nonstick coating inhibits browning of meats, but we have never found that, and the coating helps with easy cleanup.

Stock up on produce: We have two large bowls of produce sitting out all of the time. One is filled with fruit, which we use for both cooking and snacking. Lemons are a must, as they find their way into recipes for main dishes, salads, desserts, teas, and to make lemon water. Our seasoning vegetables (yellow and red onions, garlic, and shallots) live together in a second bowl. This way, we don't have to dig through a drawer or cupboard to determine what we need to buy at the store. Our kitchen is not exactly filled with light, so this approach may not work for you if you have sunlight streaming in. Store potatoes away from the onions. If stored together, the gases they give off during ripening will hasten spoilage in each other.

Keep essentials handy: We store our cooking oils, salt, and peppermill near the stove. (But not so close that they get hot.) The general advice is to store oils in a dark place to discourage rancidity, but we use them so often for sautéing and salads that they don't get a chance to degenerate. (For more information on oils, see pages 3–4.)

Use beautiful utensils: Utilitarian serving vessels get the job done. But when we use the

good-looking dishes in our everyday cooking, it lifts our spirits. These are not all top-of-the-line fare. Some of our favorite pieces are items we picked up inexpensively in European outdoor markets and American secondhand shops. Go for utensils that tell a story.

THE PANTRY

These days, every family is busy . . . we know we are not alone trying to find the time for all four of us to sit down together for at least one meal a day. But we do. One very important step is to have a stockpile of ingredients ready for cooking.

When it comes to grocery shopping, we prefer shopping every day or so to see what is at the market and let the rotating choices act as our inspiration for what to cook and serve. It puts us in close contact with our vendors, who have come to know our likes (and dislikes). We love it when our butcher says, "We just cut some hanger steak," or our wine purveyor lets us know when a shipment of our favorite Chianti has arrived. The farmer's market, of course, is a constant source of surprises and treats.

Here are the dry goods that we are never without, and some tips on how to purchase, store, and use them. We've arranged them in a somewhat random "order of importance."

Olive oil: This liquid is literally the lifeblood of Tuscan cooking, not just acting as a vehicle for cooking (sautéing) but as an actual, tangible flavor. Virtually every piece of property in the Tuscan countryside has olive trees and grapevines.

We keep two kinds of olive oil on hand, one for cooking and one for finishing. Both are extra-virgin olive oil, meaning they are from the first pressing of the olives, minimally processed, and pale green in color. Most all-purpose olive oils are moderately priced and made from a variety of olives and locations to keep the price down. Finishing oils are of the highest quality, and come from a single place, even a small estate, like fine wine. Storage is important: Sunlight encourages rancidity, so store olive oil in an opaque container or dark green bottle to keep the light out. (We use our oil so rapidly that we sometimes make an exception to this rule.)

Cooking olive oil should be relatively inexpensive. Many Mediterranean countries make very good olive oil, so the origin doesn't make a huge difference. (We know our Italian friends may squawk at this, but it's true. Italy makes about 20 percent of the world's olive oil and a single country can't handle the global demand, anyway.) Just because a brand has an Italian name doesn't mean it is Italian. Look at the oil's label and you will see a relatively self-explanatory abbreviation designating the country of origin (IT for Italy, GR for Greece, FR for France, and so on). We buy our everyday olive oil in two-liter cans, and the metal shuts out the light out so effectively that we leave it sitting out on our kitchen counter for easy access.

Finishing olive oil adds a fillip of deep flavor to a finished dish just before serving—only a few teaspoons are needed per person. We keep a top-quality Italian olive oil for this purpose, using it for pasta, vegetable side dishes, and much more. Finishing olive oil will be labeled with its precise geographic origin, usually a small region (such as Tuscany or Umbria), and preferably a specific estate (we like Laudemio or Badia a Coltibuono, among others). The olives used for finishing oils are limited in quantity and high in quality, so the oils are on the pricey side.

Olive oil, like wine, is seasonal, and the olive crush occurs in the fall. Because olive oil is delicate and ages quickly, pay attention to the use-by dates, especially for finishing oil. Oil purchased early in the year is usually from the latest crop, and, with proper storage, it will last for about six months. But again, we use ours up well before that time period passes, so we can only pass on what we've heard!

Pasta: We have strong feelings about this basic food. We think that everyone knows how to buy and cook pasta, but . . . not.

First, go Italian. Even though Americans have great wheat, and pasta is made from durum wheat, the Italian machinery makes superior dough for pasta that absorbs sauce better. And Italian pasta is usually more forgiving when you are cooking it to that perfect al dente state, and it is somehow harder to overcook. We can't prove this scientifically, but we eat a lot of pasta in our house and stand by our observation.

Next, be sure to use lots of water—at least three quarts per pound. Always salt the water. How much salt? We never measure, and just stir in enough salt to make the water taste mildly salty. But if we did measure, it would probably be about one teaspoon per quart.

Add the pasta gradually to the boiling water, stirring to keep it from sticking together, and to keep the water boiling as best as you can. If necessary, you can put the lid on the pot for a minute to help bring back the temperature, but otherwise, do not cook the pasta covered. And never add oil to the water. All that does is slick the surface when the pasta is drained, and keep the sauce from clinging.

As for the difference between fresh and dried pasta, it is not a question of one being better than the other. In this book, we share the recipes that we cook over and over again in our daily lives. Where pasta is concerned, that means dried pasta. For special occasions, we might make or buy fresh pasta. But there are no recipes that require fresh pasta.

Canned tomatoes: We have very few canned goods in our kitchen, but we make an exception for tomatoes (and beans). Honestly, outside of the few weeks when they are at their summertime peak and savored in salads, canned are simply better than fresh.

We are very picky about canned or packaged crushed or chopped tomatoes. Our favorite brand, Pomì, is sold in aseptic packaging. Their delicious Italian tomatoes are processed to the perfect texture, not too coarse or too smooth.

You can also puree whole canned tomatoes yourself, which gives you more control over their texture. Simply pour the tomatoes and their juices into a blender and pulse until you get the consistency you want, from chunky to smooth. Do not use a food processor as the juices may run out of the central hole in the chopping bowl. You can also process the tomatoes directly in the can with an immersion blender—just use a little caution to avoid splashing the juices all over. For a more rustic look you can do what Nonna Lola does: Pour the tomatoes in a bowl and crush them by hand to the preferred size and texture.

We also like canned *San Marzano tomatoes*, from that region of Campania not far from Naples. Their meaty texture, even color, and rounded flavor are worth the extra price. San Marzano tomatoes are usually packed in tomato juice with just a single sprig of basil, so they are consistent from brand to brand. Other varieties are sometimes flavored with a bunch of stuff that we don't want (garlic, chilies, and such), so look carefully to be sure that you are buying what you want.

Vinegar: Most cooks underestimate the role of acidity in flavor. A splash of lemon juice or vinegar can do wonders to perk up a dish. We always have *red wine* and *white wine vinegars* in our pantry. For the best quality, check the label and choose a vinegar that has been naturally fermented from wine, and not inoculated with bacteria to speed up the process. Most imported brands are naturally fermented.

Balsamic vinegar: Although this vinegar is very popular throughout the United States, its use in Italy is centered in the Emilia-Romagna region around Bologna and Modena. In the last few years, although they are not well known yet, some Tuscan estates are producing some extremely good ones. Most Americans know the factory-made balsamic vinegar sold at supermarkets. True *balsamico* is an artisanal product, made in small batches from sweet trebbiano grapes. It takes years to make and is portioned out, drop by drop, as a condiment for simple dishes like sautéed veal or fresh strawberries. We don't use balsamic vinegar often, but when we do, we use a middle-of-the-road version.

Canned beans: We are never without canned beans. When we have the time to cook dried beans from scratch, we will. Otherwise, when we want a starchy addition to a side dish or main course, we just open a can. Cannellini (also called white kidney) are our workhorse, but for a brown bean, try the Roman (aka cranberry or borlotti) variety. Just drain them, rinse off the canning liquid, drain again, and put to good use.

Polenta: Coarsely ground yellow cornmeal, polenta is a staple of Northern Italian cooking that is now becoming better known throughout the country. It is rib-sticking, warm comfort food, perfect to soak up the sauce from stews. Gabriele's grandmother, who is from Venice, cooks with it in our family. Traditional polenta takes forever to cook—about 45 minutes (or much longer!) of pretty constant stirring (with exploding bubbles of boiling cornmeal that can literally take the skin off your arm if you do not pay attention). We prefer instant polenta, which is ready in about five minutes.

Rice: We make a lot of risotto at home, a dish that is every bit as versatile as pasta. It is important to have the correct rice for risotto, and that means a medium-grain variety with lots of starch that helps thicken the broth into a sauce. Arborio is the most common kind and is found at almost every supermarket, but also look for carnaroli and vialone nano rice, which are even starchier. For everyday cooking, we are big fans of long-grain American rice, prepared in a rice cooker.

Farro: In a simpler world, there would be one kind of farro. There are actually three varieties (einkorn, emmer, and spelt), as well as three distinct ways of processing the grain for sale (whole grain with all of the bran, pearled with all bran removed, semi-pearled with some remaining bran). They all have different cooking times. Most farro sold in this country is semi-pearled, and ready after about twenty minutes of cooking. Always check the labeling to see the recommended cooking time and adjust the recipe accordingly.

Salt: Kosher salt gets a lot of recommendations, but really, we think that is because its coarse crystals read well on film and TV, showering down on the food. It's not a bad salt in the least. But Gabriele grew up with *sea salt*, and that's what we prefer.

We always have three containers of sea salt next to the stove. While they taste similar, they have distinct crystal sizes and shapes and feel different when eating. *Fine sea salt* has the smallest crystals, and we use that for our basic seasoning needs and baking. *Coarse sea salt* has relatively round, larger crystals. It is reserved for salting cooking water for pasta and vegetables because large crystals are easier to grab by the small handful and toss into a large pot of water. The two kinds of sea salt are sold next to each other at the market, so check and be sure you are buying the right size. (A common French brand, La Baleine, sells the fine salt in a blue container, and the coarse salt in a red one.)

Flaky sea salt, such as the British one harvested in Maldon, is a finishing salt, sprinkled over a dish just before serving. Its large, flat crystals melt slowly on the tongue, adding intriguing texture and an extra measure of seasoning.

Pepper: We only use freshly ground black pepper. Have a sturdy, reliable peppermill that holds a good amount of peppercorns—small peppermills are worthless because you always seem to be running out of pepper mid-grind. Tellicherry is a good, aromatic, and not-too-hot peppercorn that is widely available.

Hot red pepper flakes: These are actually dried chile flakes, and not black pepper at all. Italians call them *peperoncini*. You might see them labeled "crushed red pepper" at the supermarket. A pinch of these hot spicy flakes goes a long way to adding a spike of heat to food.

Spices: We never use dried herbs (see Herbs, page 10). But we will use dried spices (seeds, barks, roots, or other flavored parts of plants) because their quality does not diminish when they are dried and in most cases the flavor actually intensifies. Store them in a cool, dry place and use within six months of purchase.

Bread crumbs: No Italian kitchen is without a stash of bread crumbs for cooking. We always have a loaf of Gabriele's crusty bread in the kitchen, and that means that we occasionally end up with stale bread. (We say "occasionally" because between breakfast, lunch, dinner, sandwiches, toast, it is usually used up.) In that case, we just whirl the hard bread in a blender until it makes fine crumbs. (If the bread is on the soft side, the crumbs will be larger, and that's okay too.) Put the crumbs in a zippered plastic bag and store them in the freezer—they don't need defrosting. Or purchase plain dried bread crumbs without any additional seasonings. You can buy them for a very reasonable price at your local Italian bakery.

Pine nuts: These small, pale nuts add a buttery crunch to foods. The important thing is to know their origin (usually marked on the label), and to buy Italian or other Mediterranean nuts for the best flavor and also for safety reasons. Some people have an odd reaction to Asian pine nuts, so if your mouth has any numbness or strange sensations after eating them, don't panic. Stored in the refrigerator or freezer, pine nuts will stay fresh for about six months.

Toasting pine nuts brings out their flavor and crisps them too. To toast pine nuts, heat a small skillet over medium heat. Add the nuts and cook, stirring occasionally, until they are toasted light brown, 2 to 3 minutes. Immediately transfer the nuts to a plate to stop cooking, and let them cool before using.

Anchovies: We use anchovies to add salty flavor to lots of recipes, and most of the time, our guests don't even know they are there! Buy the small cans of anchovy fillets in olive oil. You

will rarely use all of the anchovies in one recipe. Transfer leftover anchovies and oil to a small covered container, cover with additional oil, and refrigerate them for up to two weeks.

Capers: While you can find dry, salted capers at some Italian delicatessens, we prefer the ease of use (dried capers need to be soaked) and flavor of jarred capers in brine. Just give the capers a quick rinse under cold running water to refresh them.

Flour: We use unbleached all-purpose flour in our kitchen for all of our basic cooking and baking needs. We measure our flour by the dip-and-sweep method, with 140 grams per cup.

THE FRIDGE

Our refrigerator is stocked with the perishables that every family needs. It is the abundance of Italian ingredients that make it different from most others we've seen.

Cheese: Italians truly identify with their local cheeses. For example, you will find fresh mozzarella all over Sicily, but it isn't as prevalent in Tuscany. Parmigiano-Reggiano is used most in central and northern Italy, and the closer you get to Rome, Pecorino Romano takes over the role as a grating cheese. Here are the cheeses we use the most.

Parmigiano-Reggiano: Don't call it Parmesan! Parmesan is a generic term for any old grating cheese, and not the true Parmigiano-Reggiano. The real thing is from Parma, Italy, and made from cow's milk. Standard "Parm" can be made anywhere in the world, from Wisconsin to Argentina, and it is nothing like the nutty, salty, slightly crystallized wonder of a cheese we love and cook with virtually every day. The authen-

tic version has "Parmigiano" stamped in brown letters on its straw-yellow rind.

Why is Parmigiano so special? It has umami, a "fifth flavor" component that most other cheeses lack. Buy Parmigiano in wedges and grate it yourself just before using. We love our cheese microplane, but note that the holes on the cheese-specific model are larger than the citrus zester. Also, an old-fashioned box grater works well too.

Never throw away the Parmigiano rind. Tossed into sauces, soups, and especially risotto, it can be simmered to slightly melt and give off its flavor. Remove the unmelted rind before serving the food.

Pecorino: Pecorino refers to sheep's milk cheese. *Pecorino Romano* (historically from Rome and its surrounding region, but also made in Sardinia) is aged and hard enough to grate. It has a sharp, salty taste that complements boldly flavored ingredients. Locatelli is a common brand that you will probably find in your supermarket. Like Parmigiano, it is best to buy it in chunks and grate it as needed. *Pecorino Toscano* is a fresh and moist semisoft cheese. We mainly use it as an appetizer cheese, with pear and honey, or in sandwiches with traditional cold cuts like prosciutto, soppressata, or capocollo.

Mozzarella: This smooth cheese is revered for its melting properties and for its wonderful milky flavor when eaten fresh. Low-moisture mozzarella, with its rubbery texture and bland taste, is sold at every market, but we pass it by. The commercial "fresh" mozzarella is a little better, but truthfully, it is still factory-made and a far cry from what we know as "real" mozzarella.

Hold out for handmade fresh mozzarella, sold at top-quality cheese stores and Italian delicatessens. If you can find mozzarella made with water buffalo milk (*mozzarella di bufala*, usually imported from Sicily), it is worth the price. Handmade fresh mozzarella is about the size of a large navel orange, and pretty perishable, so only buy it a day or two before using. Because it is so soft, freeze the mozzarella for an hour or so to firm it up before shredding.

Mozzarella is now sold in various sizes, including the cherry-sized *ciliegine* (a good size for salads) and the egg-shaped *ovolini* (perfect for individual servings). *Burrata* is a mozzarella ball filled with a mix of cream and shredded mozzarella that is called *stracciatella*. Stracciatella actually has many culinary meanings in Italy (see pages 57 and 249.)

Fontina: From Northern Italy, Fontina Val d'Aosta is a very creamy, smooth melting cheese with an earthy flavor that reminds some people of mushrooms. Although you will find other cheeses with similar names (such as *fontinella* or *fontal*), they are not the real thing, which is made by a consortium and encased in a brownish rind. In a pinch, the knockoff cheeses (or even Danish fontina with its red wax exterior) will do, but once you have true Fontina Val d'Aosta, you will easily notice the distinction.

Mascarpone: This soft and spreadable fresh cheese is reminiscent of crème fraîche or sour cream, except it is not as tangy. Although there are domestic versions, we prefer the imported Italian one, which comes in 8.8-ounce containers. It does not keep very well once opened, so serve it a few days after its first use.

Other Dairy: We only drink *whole milk*; we just don't like the flavor of the reduced-fat versions. Also, we believe that our bodies need some fat, just not too much. We use *unsalted butter* because that way we can control the amount of salt in the recipe.

Cured Meats: Italians are masters at curing (salting and aging) meats to preserve them. Most are made from pork. They are sometimes served as cold cuts, but we use them in our cooking too. With the exception of prosciutto di Parma, because of the laws regarding importing meats, these are all made in America with traditional Italian recipes.

Guanciale and lardo are considered specialty products at this point in time, but you will find them at top Italian delicatessens. Look for suppliers in your area with an online search. Pancetta and prosciutto are available at supermarkets. A few years ago, pancetta was unheard of, but now you can buy diced pancetta (and prosciutto) for cooking at Trader Joe's from coast to coast. (One cup of ¼-inch-diced cured pork weighs about 4 ounces.) We have no doubt that guanciale and lardo will be having their moments in the spotlight very soon.

Guanciale (cured pork jowl) is probably Gabriele's favorite cured meat for cooking as it has a good proportion of meat to fat. When cooked, its rich fat melts and deliciously seasons the food. The fresh jowl is coated with herbs, spices, and salt, and cured for a few months. The curing evaporates much of the moisture in the meat, intensifying the flavor.

Pancetta is made from cured pork belly, and it is a good substitute for guanciale. However, pancetta isn't aged as long or is as heavily spiced, so it is lighter in flavor than guanciale. The belly is rolled into a cylinder, but it can be unrolled (*pancetta tesa*) where it will look (although not taste) a lot more like American bacon. Note that bacon is smoked and has sugar in its cure, while pancetta and guanciale are only cured and unsweetened. Most of the pancetta made in the United States is rolled. You can buy it sliced or whole at Italian delicatessens, and you can sometimes find it diced and ready for cooking.

Lardo is, as its name implies, pork back fat cured with salt, herbs, and spices, and ivory white with no meat. We usually drape *lardo* on top of hot food so it can gently soften, if not melt, from the heat.

Prosciutto, made from pork leg, is considered one of the best Italian cured meats. While it can be used in cooking its slightly nutty flavor and silky texture really shine when eaten unadorned. There are domestic versions, but we prefer the imported prosciutto di Parma. Prosciutto is usually sold sliced, but a diced version for cooking is also available.

Sliced cured meats will only keep in the refrigerator for a few days. Purchased in large pieces and covered with plastic wrap, they can be refrigerated for a few weeks, guanciale even longer. (But you will need an electric meat slicer for paper-thin prosciutto, a machine that is not an option for most home cooks.)

Herbs: Outside of the occasional bay leaf, we never use dried herbs because drying evaporates the leaves' aromatic oils and alters the natural flavors. We use *thyme, basil,* and *rosemary,* on practically a daily basis, with *mint* and *sage* making occasional appearances. During the summer, we plant herbs on our deck in pots so we have them right outside the kitchen door. Otherwise, we buy them in bunches as needed at the market. You may notice that oregano is missing from this list. What can we say? We don't like it and Gabriele thinks it makes every-

thing taste like pizza. Maybe it is necessary for Southern Italian cooking, but we specialize in Tuscan cooking, where it is definitely not considered essential.

One herb that we love, and we think you should get to know, is *nipitella.* This is a Tuscan favorite, and many cooks there insist on using it in their mushroom dishes. It is as hearty as a weed, and we have a huge plant that grows up our wall at our farm in Fiesole. (It flourishes in a planter in Brooklyn too.) Its flavor combines mint and thyme. We strongly recommend that you plant *nipitella* in your garden too. It is not available as a cut herb at markets . . . yet. (We remember when you couldn't get pancetta, and now it is at our local supermarket.)

You can find *nipitella* plants and seeds at specialty herb nurseries, such as Well-Sweep Herb Farm (www.wellsweep.com) and Valley Seed Company (www.valleyseedco.com). Note that *nipitella* is often slightly misspelled in the United States, so look for it under its botanical name, *Calamintha nepeta,* or common name, lesser calamint, to be sure you are buying the right thing.

Store fresh herbs in their plastic containers (or wrapped loosely in paper towels) in the produce drawer. Fresh basil is notoriously hard to store after harvesting, as the cold air of the refrigerator turns the leaves black. To keep basil fresh for a couple of days, stand the stems in a glass of water, and cover the bunch loosely with a plastic bag. Another tip for basil (and truthfully, most fresh herbs): Always chop or slice them at the last minute, as they turn brown when the cut surfaces are exposed to the air. And use a very sharp knife for clean cuts.

Spelucchino curvo

Spelucchino dritto

Coltello trinciante da verdure

Coltello da disosso grande

Coltello trinciante da carni

Coltello filetto

Coltello trinciante

Coltello da arrosto

Coltello da pasta

Coltello da pesce

Coltello da pane

Affilatore

ANTIPASTI

OVEN-BARBECUED CHICKEN WINGS

Ali di pollo in agrodolce

• •

Makes 4 to 6 servings

G: *Over the years I noticed how Americans love chicken wings, especially at Super Bowl time. I didn't grow up with sweetness in main courses, so it took me some time to come around to barbecued chicken. In my version, I skip the ketchup and add some balsamico, peach preserves, and a splash of bourbon. I have to allow about a pound per person when I make them for dinner—they are that popular at our house.*

D: *I never considered myself a chicken-wing person until I had these. They are so tasty, and perfect for entertaining. And our kids love them.*

SAUCE
2 tablespoons unsalted butter
½ medium yellow onion, chopped
2 garlic cloves, minced
1 cup tomato puree (preferably homemade in a
    blender from canned plum tomatoes)
½ cup peach preserves
⅓ cup balsamic vinegar
¼ cup bourbon
2 tablespoons honey
1 tablespoon Dijon mustard
1 teaspoon hot red pepper sauce

CHICKEN
2 teaspoons sweet paprika
1½ teaspoons sea salt
1 teaspoon dried thyme
1 teaspoon freshly ground black pepper
¼ teaspoon cayenne pepper
4 pounds chicken wingettes
2 tablespoons extra-virgin olive oil

1. To make the sauce: Melt the butter in a medium heavy-bottomed saucepan over medium heat. Add the onion and cook, stirring occasionally, until golden brown, about 5 minutes. Stir in the garlic and cook until fragrant, about 1 minute. Stir in the tomato puree, peach preserves, balsamic vinegar, bourbon, honey, mustard, and hot red pepper sauce and bring to a simmer. Reduce the heat to low and simmer, stirring often, until thickened and reduced by about one quarter, 25 to 35 minutes. Remove from the heat and let cool.

2. Position racks in the center and top third of the oven and preheat the oven to 425°F.

3. To prepare the chicken: Mix the paprika, salt, thyme, black pepper, and cayenne pepper in a small bowl. Toss the chicken and oil in a large bowl to coat. Sprinkle with the spice mixture and toss again. Divide the wingettes between 2 large rimmed baking sheets.

4. Bake for 20 minutes. Remove from the oven and flip the wingettes over. Switch the positions of the baking sheets from top to bottom and continue baking until the wings are golden brown, about 20 minutes more. Transfer the wingettes to a large heatproof bowl. Add the sauce and stir gently to coat the wingettes. Pour off the fat from the sheets. Return the wingettes to a single sheet.

5. Bake until the sauce is glazed, 5 to 10 minutes. Transfer the wingettes and sauce to a platter and serve.

BAKED OYSTERS LIVORNESE

Ostriche alla Livornese

••••••••••••••••••••••••••••••••

Wine Pairing: Vernaccia or prosecco
Makes 3 to 4 servings

Livorno is not a big tourist destination, except maybe for the Florentines who drive the fifty-mile distance to buy the freshest, most delicious fish and shellfish. We often make the trip to enjoy a day at the beach and the marvelous seafood restaurants. These oysters are a specialty at these seaside eateries, broiled with an herbed crumb topping that allows the meat to stay plump and juicy.

TOPPING

⅓ cup plain dried bread crumbs
2 tablespoons extra-virgin olive oil, as needed
2 tablespoons finely chopped fresh flat-leaf
  parsley
1 tablespoon finely chopped shallot
2 garlic cloves, minced

2 teaspoons fresh lemon juice
Sea salt and freshly ground black pepper

12 oysters, shucked, with the meat returned to
  the deeper halves of their shells
Lemon wedges, for serving

1. Position the broiler rack about 6 inches from the source of heat and preheat the broiler on high. Crumple a large sheet or two of aluminum foil to fit onto a standard rimmed baking sheet, creating pockets to hold the oysters upright during cooking. (A standard baking sheet, about 10 by 14 inches, will fit more easily into most broilers than a larger, half-sheet pan.)

2. To make the topping: Combine the bread crumbs, oil, parsley, shallot, garlic, and lemon juice in a small bowl. Season to taste with salt and pepper.

3. Divide the topping evenly over the oysters in their shells. Securely nestle the oysters, crumbed side up, in the crumpled foil. Broil the oysters until the topping is browned, 3 to 5 minutes. Serve immediately with the lemon wedges.

TIP There are many ways to keep the oysters from rocking on the baking sheet. Some cooks use rock salt, which is only sold in large amounts. The crumpled foil trick works very well and saves you a trip to the hardware store.

ROASTED OLIVES WITH LEMON, GARLIC, AND HERBS

Olive scottate

••

Wine Pairing: Whatever you want, from Chianti to prosecco
Makes 6 to 8 servings

Olive trees are everywhere in Tuscany, and they are traditionally used for oil production and not eating. These olives are relatively small with concentrated flavor. So, the olives used for appetizers are actually from Southern Italy, where the olives are also cured and eaten. Cured olives came on the ships with the Italian immigrants, as preserved olives would not spoil on the long trip. For the best color and flavor, look for two relatively new varieties. Cerignola, from Puglia, are big and meaty and come in intense red, green, and black hues. Sicilian Castelvetrano are smaller but equally tasty and have a pretty green color. A quick roasting with a few seasonings infuses them with herbaceous flavor.

2 tablespoons extra-virgin olive oil	1 pound olives, such as Cerignola and
Six 3-inch sprigs fresh thyme	Castelvetrano, in assorted sizes and colors
Two 3-inch sprigs fresh rosemary	(about 3 cups)
½ teaspoon coarsely crushed fennel seeds	½ lemon, cut into ¼-inch rounds
¼ teaspoon hot red pepper flakes	1 large garlic clove, unpeeled and crushed

1. Position a rack in the center of the oven and preheat the oven to 400°F.

2. Stir and crush the oil, thyme, rosemary, fennel seeds, and red pepper flakes together in a baking dish large enough to hold the olives in a single layer. (A terra-cotta baking dish or a ceramic quiche pan are both good options.) Stir in the olives and lemon rounds.

3. Roast, stirring halfway through cooking, until the mixture is very fragrant and sizzling, about 20 minutes. During the last 5 minutes, stir in the garlic. Remove from the oven and cool until warm or at room temperature. (The olives can be covered and refrigerated for up to 5 days. Remove from the refrigerator 30 minutes before serving.)

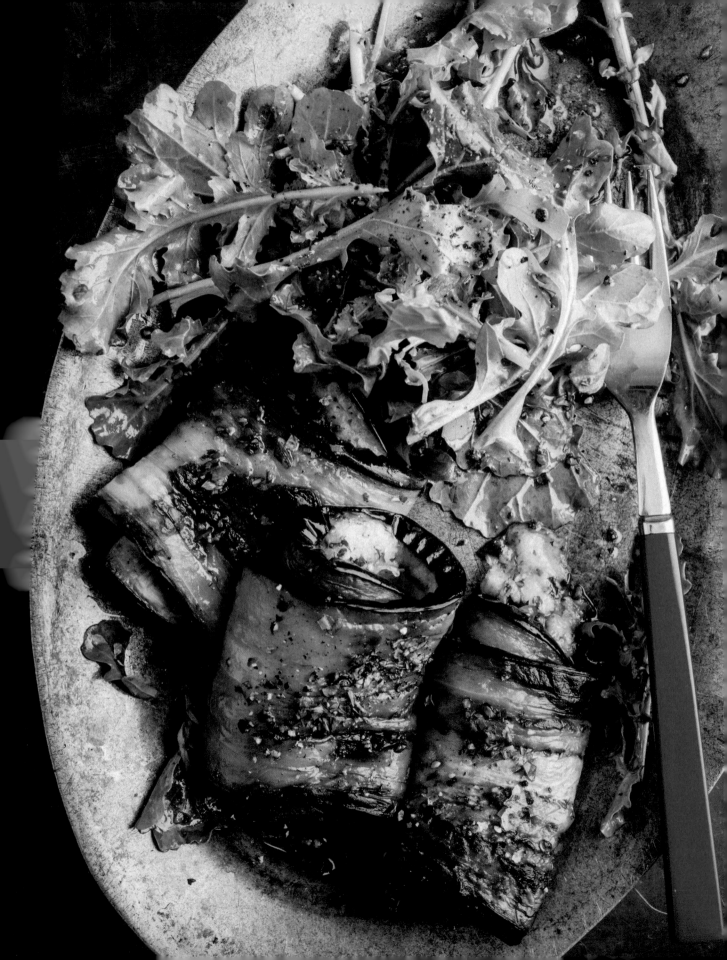

EGGPLANT ROLLS WITH HAM AND CHEESE

Involtini di melanzane

· ·

Wine Pairing: A light red, such as Nebbiolo

Makes 4 to 6 servings

G: *When traveling in Tennessee, we were struck by the similarity between the local country ham and Italian prosciutto. Both are sweet, salty, and silky at the same time. I only wish that country ham and "real" imported prosciutto di Parma were as easy to find as the smoked ham sold at every delicatessen. I used the country ham in one of my favorite dishes, Involtini di melanzane—eggplant rolled with ham and cheese. These are often prepared in the Sicilian style and baked with lots of red sauce. That's just fine for a big main course, but this version is much lighter. It is still fairly substantial, so you might want to follow it with a seafood entrée. Pecorino Toscano, a semisoft sheep cheese, is not always easy to find, so substitute fontina, if need be.*

LEMON-HERB VINAIGRETTE

3 tablespoons fresh lemon juice
1 teaspoon finely chopped fresh thyme
1 teaspoon finely chopped fresh rosemary
⅓ cup plus 1 tablespoon extra-virgin olive oil
Sea salt and freshly ground black pepper

2 small globe eggplants, about 1 pound each
¼ cup canola oil, as needed, plus more for the baking dish
1½ cups shredded semisoft Pecorino Toscano, such as Pinna Brigante
2 tablespoons coarsely chopped fresh flat-leafed parsley, plus more for serving
6 thin slices Virginia ham or prosciutto, cut in half to make 12 pieces, each about 3 inches square
Sea salt and freshly ground black pepper
5 ounces baby arugula for serving

1. To make the vinaigrette: Whisk the lemon juice, thyme, and rosemary in a small bowl. Gradually whisk in the oil. Season to taste with salt and pepper. Cover and store at room temperature for up to 4 hours.

2. Using a thin sharp knife, trim off and discard the rounded "shoulders" of each eggplant, as they are too small to roll properly. Cut the remaining eggplant lengthwise into 12 slices about ⅓ inch thick. Heat the canola oil in a large skillet over high heat until it is hot but not smoking. In batches, add the eggplant and cook, turning once, until pliable and lightly browned, about 2 minutes. Add more oil to the skillet, as needed, being sure to heat it well before adding the eggplant. Transfer eggplant slices to a paper-towel-lined baking sheet or platter. Let the eggplant cool, turning it to drain on both sides.

3. Position a rack in the center of the oven and preheat the oven to 375°F. Lightly oil a rimmed baking sheet.

4. Mix the cheese and parsley in a medium bowl. Knead and press the mixture in your hand to make 12 equal logs (they will fall apart a little, but don't worry). Place a piece of ham on the wider end of each eggplant slice, and top with a cheese log. Starting at the covered end, roll up each eggplant slice to enclose the filling. Arrange the rolls, seam side down, on the baking sheet. Season with salt and pepper. (The eggplant rolls can be covered and kept at room temperature for up to 2 hours.)

5. Bake until the cheese begins to melt out of the rolls and the eggplant is tender, about 15 minutes. Remove from the oven.

6. Position the broiler rack about 6 inches from the source of heat and preheat the broiler on high. Broil the eggplant until they are lightly browned, 1 or 2 minutes. Remove from the broiler and let cool slightly.

7. Toss the arugula with the vinaigrette in a large bowl. Divide the arugula salad among 4 to 6 dinner plates and top each one with an equal number of rolls. Sprinkle with the parsley and serve immediately.

FOCACCIA WITH GARBANZO BEANS AND RED ONION

Focaccia di ceci e cipolla

••

Wine/Beer Pairing: Young Sangiovese or lager beer
Makes 8 to 12 pieces

There are few greater pleasures in our life than sitting around a table with a bottle of red wine and a big tray of this focaccia before dinner, sipping, chatting, and nibbling to our heart's content. It's a habit we got into on the farm in Tuscany and one that we have brought stateside. Start making this focaccia the night before, because it gets its special fluffy texture from an overnight rise in the fridge. At the very least, make the dough in the morning and refrigerate all day to make the flatbread for your early evening snack.

FOCACCIA DOUGH
1 cup cold tap water
2 tablespoons extra-virgin olive oil, plus more
   for the bowl
1½ teaspoons instant (also called bread-
   machine or quick-rise) yeast
1 teaspoon sea salt
3 cups (420 grams) unbleached bread flour, as
   needed

3 tablespoons extra-virgin olive oil, plus more
   for the plastic wrap
1 medium red onion, cut into thin half-moons
⅔ cup canned garbanzo beans (chickpeas),
   drained, rinsed, and patted dry
Flaky sea salt, such as Maldon, or kosher salt

1. To make the focaccia dough: Mix the water, oil, yeast, and salt in the bowl of a stand mixer fitted with the paddle. With the machine on low speed, gradually add enough of the flour to make a soft dough that pulls away from the sides of the bowl. Change to the dough hook and knead on medium-low speed, adding more flour as necessary, until the dough is smooth, elastic, and slightly tacky, about 8 minutes.

   To make the dough by hand: Combine the water, oil, yeast, and salt in a large bowl. Using a sturdy spoon, gradually stir in enough of the flour (about 2 cups) to make a stiff dough that can't be stirred. Transfer the dough to a well-floured work surface. Knead, adding just enough flour to keep the dough from sticking to the surface and your hands (but keeping the dough moist), until the dough is smooth, elastic, and slightly tacky, about 10 minutes.

2. Generously oil a medium bowl. Turn out the dough onto a lightly floured work surface and shape it into a ball. Add the ball to the bowl and turn to coat it with oil. Cover the bowl tightly with plastic wrap and refrigerate for at least 8 and up to 24 hours.

3. Use 1 tablespoon of the oil to generously oil a 9 by 13-inch quarter-sheet pan. Punch the dough down. Pat, stretch, and pull the dough to fit the pan, patting it to an even thickness, being sure

to fill the corners. Loosely cover the pan with oiled plastic wrap, oiled side down. Let stand in a warm place until the dough puffs up to the edge of the pan, about 1½ hours.

4. Heat 1 tablespoon of the oil in a large skillet over medium heat. Add the onion and cook, stirring occasionally, until it is tender but not browned, 5 to 7 minutes. Remove from heat and let cool.

5. Position a rack in the upper third of the oven and preheat the oven to 400°F.

6. Uncover the dough. Scatter the onion and garbanzo beans on top and gently press them into the dough. Drizzle the remaining 1 tablespoon oil on top. Bake until the dough is golden brown, 25 to 30 minutes. Sprinkle the flaky salt over the focaccia. Let cool for 10 minutes. Cut into portions and serve warm or cool completely.

BRUSCHETTA WITH MUSHROOMS AND FONTINA

Bruschetta boscaiola

• •

Wine Pairing: Chianti, of course!
Makes 8 bruschetta

Chianti goes well with so many foods, but it really is a perfect match with mushrooms. Cremini is the most flavorful supermarket variety, but feel free to try this with an assortment of mushrooms, such as enoki, stemmed shiitake caps, and oyster.

MUSHROOMS
2 tablespoons extra-virgin olive oil
10 ounces cremini mushrooms, thinly sliced
Two 3-inch sprigs fresh thyme
Two 3-inch sprigs fresh *nipitella* or mint
2 tablespoons finely chopped shallots
1 garlic clove, minced
½ cup hearty red wine, such as Chianti
Sea salt and freshly ground black pepper

4 wide slices crusty bread, about 8 inches
   across (see Note, page 30)
1 tablespoon extra-virgin olive oil, plus more
   as needed
1 cup (4 ounces) shredded fontina cheese,
   preferably Fontina Val d'Aosta
Fresh thyme leaves, for garnish

1. Position the broiler rack about 6 inches from the source of heat and preheat the broiler on high.

2. To make the mushrooms: Heat the oil in a large skillet over medium-high heat. Add the mushrooms, thyme, and *nipitella* and cook, stirring occasionally, until the mushrooms give off their juices and begin to brown, about 6 minutes. Stir in the shallot and garlic and cook, stirring occasionally, until the shallots are tender, about 2 minutes. Stir in the wine and boil until is has almost completely reduced, about 2 minutes more. Season to taste with the salt and pepper. Remove from the heat and cover to keep warm.

3. Drizzle the bread with about 1 tablespoon of the olive oil. Toast the bread in the broiler, on one side, about 1 minute. Turn the bread and very lightly toast the other side, about 30 seconds more. Divide the fontina evenly over the bread. Return to the broiler and broil until the cheese is melted and the exposed crust is toasted, about 1 minute.

4. Remove and discard the thyme and *nipitella* from the mushroom mixture. Transfer the bread to a cutting board. Top with equal amounts of the mushroom mixture. Cut each slice in half vertically to make 8 pieces and top each one with a sprinkle of thyme. Serve immediately, with a fork and knife.

BRUSCHETTA WITH ROASTED TOMATOES AND MOZZARELLA

Bruschetta con pomodori arrostiti e mozzarella

• •

Wine Pairing: Müller-Thurgau from Trentino
Makes 8 bruschetta

G: *In Tuscany, the most common bruschetta is a slice of untoasted bread topped with fresh ripe tomato and basil salad dressed with delicious young olive oil. Tradition aside, this version delivers more flavor and more substance, transforming a simple snack into an irresistible antipasti. Or serve a couple of slices per person, add a beer, and call it dinner.*

ROASTED TOMATOES

1 tablespoon extra-virgin olive oil, plus more for oiling a baking dish
8 plum (Roma) tomatoes, halved lengthwise
Sea salt and freshly ground black pepper
Two 3-inch sprigs fresh thyme

4 wide slices crusty bread (see Note, page 30), about 8 inches across, cut in half vertically to make 8 pieces
1 tablespoon extra-virgin olive oil, plus more as needed
1 large garlic clove, peeled
8 ounces fresh mozzarella, thinly sliced
8 large basil leaves

1. Position a rack in the center of the oven and preheat the oven to 300°F.

2. Lightly oil a baking dish just large enough to hold the tomatoes. Place the tomatoes, cut sides up, in the dish and season to taste with the salt and pepper. Add the thyme and drizzle with the tablespoon of oil. Bake until the tomatoes are shrunken and very tender, and their juices are thick and concentrated, about 2 hours. Remove from the oven and let cool to room temperature. Discard the thyme.

3. Position the broiler rack 6 inches from the source of heat and preheat the broiler on high.

4. Drizzle the bread with the olive oil. Toast the bread in the broiler on one side, about 1½ minutes. Turn the bread and very lightly toast the other side, about 30 seconds more. Remove the bread from the broiler and rub the more toasted side with the garlic clove. Turn over and divide the mozzarella evenly over the lightly toasted sides. Return the bread to the broiler and cook until the mozzarella melts, about 1 minute.

5. Transfer the bread to a cutting board. Tear the basil leaves into small pieces. Top each slice with 2 tomato halves, sprinkle with the basil, and serve immediately with a fork and knife.

BRUSCHETTA WITH ASPARAGUS, RICOTTA, AND GOAT CHEESE

Bruschetta di ricotta, caprino e asparagi

• •

Makes 8 bruschetta

Like many other great recipes, we created this one by accident. Cleaning out the fridge of leftovers, we made these as a snack and now it's a favorite. A grating of fresh lemon zest over the bruschetta before serving is a nice touch. You can use any kind of spreadable, rindless goat cheese (caprino).

One 5.3-ounce container spreadable goat
   cheese, such as Chavrie
½ cup ricotta cheese, preferably fresh
2 pounds thin asparagus, woody stems
   discarded
3 tablespoons extra-virgin olive oil, plus more
   as needed

4 wide slices crusty bread, about 8 inches
   across (see Note)
Flaky sea salt, such as Maldon, and freshly
   ground black pepper, for serving
1 lemon, for serving

1. Mash the goat cheese and ricotta together in a small bowl until smooth and combined. Set aside.

2. Position a rack in the center of the oven and preheat the oven to 425°F.

3. Place the asparagus on a large rimmed baking sheet. Drizzle with about 2 tablespoons of the oil and roll the asparagus in the oil. Spread the asparagus in a single layer. Roast until the asparagus is crisp-tender and lightly browned, about 12 minutes, depending on the thickness of the asparagus. Remove from the oven and let cool. Cut the spears in half crosswise to fit the bread.

4. Position the broiler rack about 6 inches from the source of heat and preheat the broiler on high.

5. Drizzle the bread with the remaining 1 tablespoon oil. Toast the bread in the broiler, turning once, until crisp and golden brown on both sides, about 2 minutes total. Remove from the broiler and let the bread cool slightly.

6. Generously spread the cheese mixture over the toasts and cut each toast in half vertically to make 8 pieces. Top with the asparagus and season to taste with the salt and pepper. Finely grate the zest from the lemon (a microplane does the best job) over the asparagus before serving.

NOTE The perfect bread for bruschetta is a wide and crusty artisan loaf, either round (*pugliese* or *boule*) or oblong (*bâtard*). In Tuscany, there are really only two loaves—unsalted Toscano, and *pugliese*, which is the same dough, only salted. Breads with what is called a "tight crumb," with fewer holes, are best. You can't make good bruschetta without good bread.

CROSTINI WITH ARTICHOKE TAPENADE

Crostini con tapenade di carciofi

• •

Wine Pairing: Rosso di Montalcino
Makes about 2½ cups tapenade; 24 crostini

D: *This spread is perfect for crostini or bruschetta, and makes use of readily available frozen artichoke hearts. I like to mix the leftovers with canned Italian tuna for an amazing sandwich filling.*

TAPENADE

1 garlic clove, crushed
2 tablespoons drained nonpareil capers
2 anchovy fillets in olive oil, drained and coarsely chopped
One 9-ounce box frozen artichoke hearts, thawed
¾ cup coarsely chopped pimento-stuffed green olives
½ cup coarsely chopped jarred roasted red bell pepper
2 tablespoons extra-virgin olive oil

1 tablespoon finely chopped fresh flat-leaf parsley, plus more for garnish
2 tablespoons fresh lemon juice
1 teaspoon minced fresh thyme
⅛ teaspoon hot red pepper flakes
2 tablespoons Mayonnaise (page 158)
Sea salt and freshly ground black pepper

CROSTINI

2 tablespoons extra-virgin olive oil, plus more for oiling baking sheet
1 long loaf crusty bread (baguette)

1. To make the tapenade: Drop the garlic through the feed tube of a food processor to mince it. Add the capers and anchovy fillets and pulse a few times to chop them. Add the artichoke hearts, olives, red bell pepper, oil, parsley, lemon juice, thyme, and red pepper flakes and pulse until the mixture is finely chopped. (You can also finely chop each of the ingredients by hand and mix them together.) Transfer to a bowl and stir in the mayonnaise. Season to taste with the salt and pepper, cover, and refrigerate for at least 2 hours and up to 2 days to blend the flavors. Remove from the refrigerator 30 minutes before serving.

2. To make the crostini: Position a rack in the center of the oven and preheat the oven to 350°F. Lightly oil a large rimmed baking sheet.

3. Using a serrated knife held at a slight diagonal, cut the bread into ¼-inch-thick slices. (The exact number of slices will depend on the length of the bread, but you should get at least 24.) Spread the slices on the prepared baking sheet and drizzle with the remaining 2 tablespoons oil. Bake until the crostini are golden brown, 12 to 15 minutes. Remove from the oven and let the crostini cool. (The crostini can be prepared up to 8 hours ahead and stored at room temperature.)

4. Transfer the tapenade to a serving bowl, sprinkle with parsley, and serve with the crostini.

OUR HOME BAR

The after-work happy hour happens every day of the workweek in Italy. While it has a centuries-old wine culture, cocktails are far from unknown. Big cities like Rome and Milan do have cocktail bars—in fact, we shared caipirinhas on our first date in Florence. In the summertime, a Negroni or Aperol spritz will do a lot to cool you off on a hot Tuscan evening.

While a bottle of wine and a plate of antipasti is a great way to show your hospitality, mixing cocktails takes a little extra effort that your guests are sure to appreciate. In all of our traveling we have found that a good bowl of pasta can be had in many places, but a really great cocktail is not so easy to find outside of the United States.

The Italian approach to drinking is ingrained in their day-to-day existence. An Italian family has two bars in its life: one on their block and another at home. The American corner bar can be a kind of dark and forlorn place, but not the local Italian version. Invariably a prime example of the mom-and-pop business model, each bar is the center of the neighborhood, selling coffee, liquor, pastries, cigarettes, and lottery tickets, among other sundries and necessities. Advice and political arguments are free of charge.

We don't have the equivalent of this neighborhood bar in Brooklyn. In Fiesole, we can buy a carton of milk at the corner bar. It is a rare day when an Italian does not stop into the bar for a glass of wine or a shot of something stronger, either on the way to work or on the way home or both. It's like going to church—you always know what time of day you are going to be there.

Our home bar is cross-cultural, stocked with both American and Italian liquors. Italian spirits often fall into one of two very specific categories: *aperitivo* (like French *apéritif*, meant to be enjoyed before a meal, often simply on ice or with a club soda mixer) and *digestivo* (usually savored after a meal, presumably as a digestive). In both cases, they are made from complex combinations of floral, herbal, and vegetable ingredients, distilled with alcohol and balanced with a sweetener. While these liquors were surely designed to be drunk on their own, we sometimes use them as flavorful cocktail ingredients too.

We always have bottles of bourbon, vodka, and scotch to appease the old-school drinkers in our group, and a cachaça and rum for our friends who like tropical cocktails. The fridge holds a chilled bottle or two of Italian white wine, such as Vernaccia, and we always have a Tuscan red (Chianti Classico) ready to open. Vodka and limoncello are usually stored in the freezer so we can take ice-cold shots.

Here is a list of the Italian liquors that we always have in our bar:

Aperol (*aperitivo*)
Orange is the main ingredient in this *aperitivo*, with a hint of quinine (from the bark of the cinchona tree). We like to add it to chilled prosecco as our idea of the ultimate Aperol spritz, or on the rocks with an orange slice.

Averna (*digestivo*)

Amari (bitters) is a subcategory of Italian liquors named for their flavor. They are not the same as the aromatic bitters used by the drop to flavor American cocktails. Averna is one our favorites, a dark, syrupy liqueur with spicy raisin flavors.

Campari (*aperitivo*)

Dark red, this liqueur has undertones of the sour orange called *chinotto*, as well as many other herbs and spices. It mixes well with soda and is required for the Negroni (equal parts gin, red vermouth, and Campari) and its cousin, The Boulevardier (page 41).

Cynar (*digestivo*)

Another *amaro*, the artichoke is one of this liquor's main ingredients. Cynar and orange juice is a very popular combination in Europe, so give it a try. The bottle label is a classic of Italian graphics, with a big, beautiful artichoke front and center.

Grappa (*digestivo*)

Distilled from the leftovers of winemaking (grape skins, seeds, and pulp), this transparent brandy is very heady, to say the least. It is the traditional after-dinner drink preferred by many of our Italian buddies, so we always have a bottle. It can be added to a shot of espresso to make *caffè corretto* ("correct coffee"). There are many producers, and the specific flavor depends on the grape and distillery locale. The smaller the producer is, the higher the price. It also can be aged, resulting in a darker and smoother drink that is a bit easier to drink neat. However, *caffè corretto* or any mixed drink is usually made with un-aged grappa.

Limoncello

This lemon-flavored liqueur is a specialty of Sorrento and Amalfi on the southwestern coast of Italy, and all the way down south into Sicily, and is becoming more readily available at American liquor stores. We also make it at home ourselves, and there are lots of recipes online (or in our first book, *Extra Virgin: Recipes and Love from Our Tuscan Kitchen*) if you want to give it a try. We also use it in the Limoncello and Mascarpone Parfaits (page 247). Drink it ice cold, either straight up (chilled beforehand in the fridge or freezer) or on the rocks. Most people drink it after dinner, like a typical liqueur, but it is also tasty as a kind of grown-up lemonade cocktail with club soda.

Prosecco

Prosecco is a sparkling white wine from northeast Italy. It is a lot less expensive than the average French Champagne, so it's a better choice as a cocktail mixer, and prosecco is the less sweet of the two. If you want to make a Bellini, definitely use prosecco for the correct Italian character. There are three levels of fizziness: *spumante* (the most bubbles), *frizzante* (only a moderate fizz), and *tranquillo* (still).

Vermouth (*aperitivo*)

A few centuries ago, winemakers discovered that increasing the alcohol content of wine (usually by adding extra brandy) lengthened the time before it spoiled, and they added flavorings to mellow the taste. (The word *vermouth* derives from the herb wormwood, an ingredient in the original recipe.) Two different vermouths evolved. The first, made with red wine in Italy by the Carpano family in the late 1700s, is now known as *sweet vermouth*. A few decades later, in France, straw-colored *dry vermouth* was developed by the herbalist Louis Noilly (later joined by his son-in-law to form the company Noilly Prat). Other variations, made by Italian and French producers, include "extra dry" and "bianco." For many decades, vermouth was only described by its country, with red Italian and dry French as the two choices. Beginning in the last quarter of the nineteenth century, both kinds of vermouth became indispensable ingredients in such classic American cocktails as the martini and Manhattan.

As far as Italian vermouths go, we don't have a strong preference. For moderately priced brands, choose either Cinzano or Martini & Rossi. Carpano's Antica Formula is boutique vermouth at a higher price, but noticeably more herbal and spicier than the others.

• • •

You don't need much in the line of bar equipment. A *cocktail shaker* is a must. We like the ones with a lid/strainer combination, as it saves us from having to use separate strainers. Remember, not all cocktails are actually shaken; many are stirred because shaking makes the drink cloudy, and sometimes a clear cocktail looks better. To that end, a *long bar spoon* (an iced-tea spoon is fine) is used. A *jigger glass* with ½-ounce increments is an essential. The best bartenders measure their ingredients for uniformity from drink to drink. Cocktail recipes are given in ounces: 1 ounce equals 2 tablespoons. And it goes without saying that you'll need a *corkscrew* and a *bottle opener*.

COCKTAILS

THE BOULEVARDIER

Bourbon Negroni

• •

Makes 1 cocktail

Many of you will recognize this drink as a variation on the Negroni. It was invented in 1920 in Venice, and within a decade, the Negroni had crossed the border and landed in Paris. There, the American expat crowd substituted bourbon for gin and dubbed it The Boulevardier, named after a short-lived magazine published by a Rockefeller scion. You can serve this straight up or on the rocks.

1½ fluid ounces bourbon
1 fluid ounce sweet vermouth

1 fluid ounce Campari
Orange slice, for garnish

Add the bourbon, sweet vermouth, and Campari to an ice-filled cocktail shaker. Stir well for about 10 seconds. Strain into a chilled martini glass. Garnish with the orange slice and serve.

LA TOSSE

Hot Bourbon Toddy

• • • • • • • • • • •

Makes 1 cocktail

D: *I believe in this drink's medicinal properties to soothe the common cold (la tosse means "the cough" in Italian). But it is too good to save for when you are under the weather. On a chilly evening, curl up with a book and this hot toddy and it is guaranteed to warm you up from the inside out.*

⅓ cup boiling water
1 tablespoon honey

½ lemon
1½ fluid ounces bourbon

Mix the boiling water and honey together in a mug to dissolve the honey. Juice the half lemon into the mug, and drop in the lemon half. Add the bourbon, stir, and sip.

ESTATE

Lavender-Bourbon Iced Tea

• • • • • • • • •

Makes 6 cocktails

In our Brooklyn garden during the summer (estate is the word for this season in Italian), we have pots of lavender, and when you brush against them, they release their aroma. Their heady fragrance inspired us to make this cocktail, which can also be made with dried lavender. Just be sure to buy culinary lavender and not the kind used for potpourri, which is often sprayed with lacquer.

LAVENDER ICED TEA

1 tablespoon fresh lavender flowers or
    1½ teaspoons edible dried lavender
3 tablespoons honey
4 bags black tea, such as English Breakfast, or
    4 teaspoons loose black tea
1 cup ice water

9 fluid ounces bourbon
6 lemon slices, for garnish
6 sprigs fresh lavender or mint, for garnish
    (optional)

1. Slowly bring 2 cups of water and the lavender to a boil in a medium saucepan over medium heat. Remove from the heat. Add the honey and stir to dissolve. Add the tea and let steep for 3 minutes—no longer or the iced tea could be bitter. Strain the tea mixture through a wire sieve into a large bowl, pressing on the solids. Add the ice water and stir. Transfer to a pitcher. Refrigerate until chilled, at least 1 hour and up to 2 days.

2. For each drink, add 1½ fluid ounces bourbon to a tall ice-filled glass. Add the iced tea (about ½ cup) and stir well. Garnish with the lemon and lavender and serve.

THE BITTER SOUTHERNER

Amaro and Bourbon Cocktail

· ·

Makes 1 cocktail

Amari, *the category of bitter Italian spirits, is a new sweetheart with American mixologists who are newly discovering its complex, herbal flavors. Averna, with its rich, spicy taste, is probably Italy's favorite* amaro, *but it doesn't have to be saved for an after-dinner drink. Give it a try in this variation on the Manhattan. Bourbon's strength works beautifully to balance the syrupy Averna.*

1½ fluid ounces Averna
1½ fluid ounces bourbon

Orange twist, for garnish

Pour the Averna and bourbon into an ice-filled cocktail glass. Stir well, add the orange twist, and serve.

THE CONGA

Mojito with Grappa

• • • • • • • • • • • • •

Makes 1 cocktail

G: *Grappa is an aggressive spirit. Sometimes, the morning after drinking one too many, my head is throbbing like a big drum—and I was a drummer for many years, so I can make the comparison. I sometimes have a small glass as an after-dinner* digestivo, *especially in the cold weather, or I'll add some to my espresso when running around doing errands. A good dry grappa also works in this variation on the mojito theme, swapping grappa for rum. The mint, soda, and sugar smooth out the liquor's rough edges. Use a moderately priced grappa for this cocktail and save single-vineyard bottles for sipping.*

D: *I never had grappa until I met Gabriele. To introduce me to it, he would make this cocktail for me.*

6 large fresh mint leaves
½ lime
2 teaspoons superfine (bartender's) sugar
1½ fluid ounces un-aged grappa

Club soda, for serving
1 lime wedge, for garnish
1 mint sprig, for garnish

Using a muddler, crush the mint leaves, lime half, and sugar in the bottom of a tall glass, working them together for at least 15 seconds. Add the grappa and stir well with a long spoon to dissolve the sugar. Fill the glass with ice and add enough club soda to fill the glass. Stir gently with the spoon to combine. Garnish with the lime wedge and mint sprig. Serve immediately.

TUSCAN MARY

Bloody Mary with Basil Vodka

• • • • • • • • • • • • • • • • • •

Makes 6 drinks

Why drink a plain old Bloody Mary when you can have our Tuscan version? The night before serving, infuse the vodka with basil. There are basil-flavored vodkas for sale, but this is very easy (and fresher tasting) to make at home. The tomato juice base has balsamic vinegar to pump up the Italian notes. Part of the fun of indulging in a "Mary" of any nationality is the garnish, so if you want to stick a cube of salami or a pitted green olive onto the skewer, be our guest. Truth be told, we are purists and prefer a big celery stick as our stirrer . . . but that's just us!

Special equipment: 6 long bamboo skewers

BASIL VODKA
12 fluid ounces (1½ cups) vodka
6 large sprigs fresh basil

TUSCAN MARY MIX
3 cups canned tomato juice
2 tablespoons balsamic vinegar
2 tablespoons fresh lemon juice
2 tablespoons prepared horseradish
½ teaspoon Worcestershire sauce
1 large pinch sea salt
1 large pinch freshly ground black pepper

GARNISH
12 cherry tomatoes
6 *ciliegine* (small mozzarella balls)
6 sprigs fresh basil

1. To make the vodka: At least 1 day before serving, combine the vodka and basil leaves in a covered jar. Refrigerate for 1 or 2 days. Strain and discard the basil. Return the vodka to the jar and refrigerate until ready to use, up to 5 days.

2. To make the mix: Whisk the tomato juice, balsamic vinegar, lemon juice, horseradish, Worcestershire sauce, salt, and pepper in a pitcher. Cover and refrigerate for at least 4 hours or up to 1 day to blend the flavors.

3. To make the garnish: Spear 2 cherry tomatoes and 1 *ciliegine* on each skewer.

4. For each serving, pour 2 fluid ounces of the vodka into an ice-filled glass. Add enough Tuscan Mary Mix (½ cup or 4 fluid ounces) to fill the glass and stir well. Add a garnished skewer and a basil sprig to the glass and serve.

LIMONCELLO DROP

Limoncello and Vodka Martini

• •

Makes 1 cocktail

We often reserve our homemade limoncello to sip as an after-dinner treat. However, we have found that it also can be turned into this sweet-tart cocktail. If you wish, skip the sugaring of the cocktail-glass rim, although it is an easy garnish that always gets guests talking.

¼ lemon
White sanding sugar (also called decorating sugar), for sugaring glass rim

2 fluid ounces vodka
1 fluid ounce limoncello
Thin lemon twist, for garnish (optional)

1. Run the lemon wedge around the rim of a chilled martini glass. Spread a few tablespoons of the sanding sugar in a saucer. Roll the outside of the glass rim in the sugar, keeping excess sugar off of the inside (just wipe it out with a clean fingertip if this happens) so the drink doesn't get too sweet. Return the remaining sugar to its container.

2. Squeeze the lemon juice from the wedge into an ice-filled shaker. Add the vodka and limoncello and stir until well chilled, about 10 seconds. Strain into the prepared glass and serve.

THE MARABOU SLIPPER

Prosecco and Campari Cocktail

••••••••••••••••••••••••••••••

Makes 1 cocktail

D: *Fizzy drinks are a lot of fun at any time of the day, but they really come into their own at brunch. The color of this drink reminds me of the night I met Gabriele. I had on pink marabou slippers. His cigarette ash fell onto the feathers and burned them! I forgave him. . . . You will get about five to six servings of this cocktail from a bottle of prosecco.*

1 fluid ounce chilled Campari

4 fluid ounces chilled prosecco, plus more as needed

Lemon twist, for garnish

Pour the Campari in a flute glass. Slowly add enough prosecco to fill the glass. Garnish with the lemon twist and serve.

SOUPS

"OLD HEN" CHICKEN SOUP

Gallina vecchia

•••••••••••••••••••••••••••••

Makes 1-quart chicken stock, plus 8 servings of chicken soup

D: *I love chicken soup and I absolutely believe that it has healing properties. Every home needs a good recipe for those days when someone in the house feels under the weather, or when you just want to serve something comforting to the family. It's a good rainy-day project because even if it seems time-consuming (without a lot of actual work), you will end up with a big batch with leftovers for freezing.*

G: *Stewing hens are literally tough old birds that do not lay eggs anymore, and putting them to a better use in the soup pot was a fact of life on the farm in Fiesole. A chicken soup made with a flavorful hen is richer than one made with a younger bird. This recipe gives a generous amount of broth to freeze for other recipes. For even deeper flavor, I always add some inexpensive chicken parts to the broth too. One last tip: Note that fresh vegetables are used for the soup itself because the ones simmered in the broth will be spent and tasteless. You will need a large stockpot to make this.*

CHICKEN STOCK

One 5-pound stewing hen (also called fowl),
    with giblets (do not use the liver in the stock)
1 pound chicken parts, such as necks, backs, or
    wings
1 medium white onion, unpeeled and cut in
    quarters
2 medium carrots, unpeeled, scrubbed, and cut
    into 1-inch chunks
3 medium celery ribs, cut into 1-inch chunks
1 garlic head, unpeeled and cut in half
    crosswise
15 fresh flat-leaf parsley stems (save the leaves
    for the soup)

CHICKEN SOUP

2 medium carrots, cut into ⅓-inch dice
2 medium celery ribs, cut into ⅓-inch dice
Sea salt and freshly ground black pepper
Finely chopped fresh flat-leaf parsley (use the
    leaves saved from the broth), for serving

1. To make the stock: Toss the whole hen, chicken parts, onion, carrots, celery, garlic, and parsley stems into the large stockpot and add enough cold water to cover them by 1 inch. Bring to a boil over high heat, skimming off any foam that rises to the surface. Reduce the heat to low. Simmer, adding hot water to the pot if needed to keep the ingredients submerged, until the chicken is tender and a wing can be easily pulled away from the body with kitchen tongs, about 2½ hours.

2. Transfer the hen to a plate, keeping the broth (with the chicken parts and vegetables) at a simmer. Let the hen cool until easy to handle, at least 15 minutes. Pull off the meat from the chicken,

loosely cover with plastic wrap, and refrigerate until ready to use. Return the skin and bones to the stock and continue simmering until the stock is full flavored, about 1 hour more.

3. Line a colander with a couple of layers of wet, squeezed-dry cheesecloth. Strain the stock into another large pot, discarding the solids. Let the stock stand for a few minutes. Skim some (but not all) of the clear yellow fat that rises to the surface. Measure and reserve 2 quarts of the stock. (The remaining stock can be cooled, covered, and refrigerated for up to 3 days or frozen for up to 3 months.)

4. To make the soup: Rinse the stockpot. Pour the reserved stock back into the pot. Add the diced carrots and celery and bring it to a simmer over medium heat. Cook until the vegetables are tender, about 20 minutes. Using your fingers, shred the cooled chicken meat into bite-sized pieces. During the last few minutes of cooking, stir the meat into the soup. Season to taste with the salt and pepper. Ladle into bowls, sprinkle with the parsley, and serve hot.

TIP Look for stewing hens (fowl) at large supermarkets, especially during the Jewish holidays of Passover and Rosh Hashanah when homemade chicken soup is considered essential fare. They are also sold at Chinese or Latino markets on a year-round basis. If you just can't find a stewing hen, substitute a standard chicken. In that case, because it is much more tender, only simmer the bird for about 1 hour, or until the wing pulls away easily from the joint. Continue with the rest of the recipe as directed, simmering the skin and bones, but not the meat, until the broth is rich and full flavored, about 1 hour.

ITALIAN EGG DROP SOUP

Stracciatella

• •

Makes 4 cups

You hardly need a recipe for this super-easy soup. However, like all simple dishes, there are good versions and even better ones. Make this with homemade stock and farm-fresh eggs from the farmer's market and you will see why it is one of Italy's most famous soups. If you see a similarity to Chinese egg drop soup, you are right.

4 cups Chicken Stock (page 55)
Sea salt and freshly ground black pepper
2 large eggs

Finely chopped fresh flat-leaf parsley, for
serving

1. Bring the stock to a boil in a medium saucepan over high heat. Reduce the heat to medium so the stock is at a brisk simmer. Season to taste with the salt and pepper.

2. Crack the eggs into a small bowl. Add a pinch of salt and a grind of pepper and whisk until combined. Stirring the stock with the whisk, pour in the eggs in a steady stream. Stop stirring and let cook until the egg mixture forms a softly set "raft" on top of the stock, about 1 minute. Ladle into bowls, sprinkle with the parsley, and serve hot.

COD AND FENNEL SOUP

Zuppa di merluzzo e finocchio

• •

Makes 6 servings

G: *There are many soups that simmer for hours, but not this one. It is a tasty example of the brothy fish soups of Italy, studded with chunks of fresh seafood. While we've chosen to use firm white cod here, you could go with other non-oily fish, such as snapper or grouper. Fennel is an important component of this soup, and if you want to increase the amount of anise flavor, substitute the parsley garnish with chopped fennel fronds. The* fettunta *sets it all off beautifully.*

D: *Our kids love this soup because it is has the simple, tomato-laced flavors they love and big chunks of not-too-fishy cod. Also, they get to have* fettunta, *and who doesn't like garlic bread?*

3 tablespoons extra-virgin olive oil
1 medium yellow onion, chopped
½ small bulb fennel, cut into ¼-inch dice (about 1 cup)
2 tablespoons finely chopped fresh flat-leaf parsley, plus more for serving
2 garlic cloves, minced
¼ teaspoon hot red pepper flakes

1 cup dry white wine, such as Pinot Grigio
One 28-ounce can tomatoes, drained, tomatoes coarsely chopped
Sea salt and freshly ground black pepper
1 pound cod fillet, skinless and cut into bite-sized pieces
Tuscan Country Toast (page 59), rubbed with garlic

1. Heat the oil in a large saucepan over medium heat. Add the onion, fennel, parsley, garlic, and red pepper flakes and cook, stirring often, until the onion begins to brown, about 4 minutes. Add the wine and cook until it is almost evaporated, about 3 minutes. Stir in the tomatoes and cook until they give off some juices, about 2 minutes.

2. Add 5 cups of water and bring to a simmer over high heat. Season to taste with the salt and black pepper. Reduce the heat to low and simmer until it is full flavored, about 30 minutes.

3. Increase the heat to medium to bring the broth to a stronger simmer. Stir in the cod and cook just until it begins to look opaque, about 3 minutes. Remove from the heat. Ladle the soup into bowls. Sprinkle each serving with more chopped parsley and serve hot with the *fettunta*.

TUSCAN COUNTRY TOAST

Fettunta

• •

Makes 4 toasts

A masterpiece of Tuscan understatement, fettunta *is just crusty toasted bread doused with olive oil, preferably a young estate variety. Sometimes the toast is rubbed with a garlic clove for extra flavor to make the best garlic bread this side of Firenze. The toast's name comes from* fetta *(slice) and* unta *(oiled). It can be served as an appetizer, plain, or topped with cooked vegetables (such as braised kale), but it is especially good as a crisp go-to with hot soups. The garlic is optional, but . . . why not?*

4 wide slices crusty bread (see Note, page 30)
2 garlic cloves (optional)

2 tablespoons extra-virgin olive oil, preferably high-quality finishing oil, plus more as needed

1. Position the broiler rack about 6 inches from the source of heat and preheat the broiler on high.

2. Toast the bread in the broiler, turning once, until crisp and golden brown on both sides, about 2 minutes. If desired, rub the garlic cloves onto the toasts—the crispy toasted edges will act as a rasp to shred the garlic onto the bread. Cut each slice in half vertically, if desired, to make 8 pieces. Drizzle with the oil and serve.

MUSSEL CHOWDER

Zuppa cremosa di cozze

• • • • • • • • • • • • • • • • • • • •

Wine Pairing: Pinot Grigio
Makes 6 servings

G: *Over the last decade, while traveling through the United States, I fell in love with clam chowder. After tasting quite a few bowls of this New England classic, I have come to know what makes a really good chowder—not too much pork, lots of mollusks, a delicious broth that is creamy and not too thick. I was inspired to develop a version that connects my new favorite to my heritage, and I started by substituting the clams with mussels. Generally cheaper than clams, mussels are a staple in Italian fish soups, so their cost makes this an everyday kind of soup instead of something to make for special occasions. One of my favorite lunches is a big bowl of this soup,* fettunta, *and a cold glass of Pinot Grigio.*

2 pounds mussels, preferably Prince Edward Island, beards removed (see Tip, page 62)
½ cup dry white wine
3 cups Vegetable Broth (page 67), plus more as needed
2 large Yukon Gold potatoes, peeled and cut into ½-inch cubes (about 12 ounces)
1 tablespoon extra-virgin olive oil
½ cup (¼-inch) diced pancetta
1 small yellow onion, finely chopped

1 small celery rib, finely chopped
1 small carrot, finely chopped
1 garlic clove, minced
½ teaspoon finely chopped fresh thyme
3 tablespoons unbleached all-purpose flour
Sea salt and freshly ground black pepper
½ cup heavy cream
Tuscan Country Toast (page 59), rubbed with garlic, for serving

1. Scrub the mussels under cold running water and put them in a large bowl. Add salted ice water to cover and let stand for about an hour or so. (This helps the mussels expel any grit from their insides.) Drain and rinse well. Discard any opened or cracked mussels.

2. Put the mussels and wine in a large pot and cover. Bring to a boil over high heat. Cook, shaking the pot occasionally, just until the mussels have opened, about 5 minutes. Remove from the heat. Using kitchen tongs, transfer the mussels to a large bowl, discarding any unopened mussels. Strain the cooking liquid through a fine mesh sieve into another bowl, leaving any grit behind in the pot. Measure the cooking liquid and add enough broth to make 4 cups. Set the cooking liquid mixture aside.

3. Meanwhile, put the potatoes in a medium saucepan and add cold salted water to cover. Bring to a boil over high heat. Reduce the heat to low and simmer until the potatoes are tender, about 25 minutes. Drain and set the potatoes aside.

4. Meanwhile, heat the oil in a large pot over medium heat. Add the pancetta and cook, stirring occasionally, until browned, about 5 minutes. Add the onion, celery, carrot, garlic, and thyme. Cover and cook, stirring occasionally, until the vegetables soften, about 3 minutes. Sprinkle in the flour and mix well. Stir in the reserved liquid mixture and bring to a simmer. Adjust the heat to medium low and cook, with the lid ajar, for 10 minutes to blend the flavors. Season to taste with the salt and pepper.

5. Stir in the cream and return to a simmer. Add the mussels and potatoes and cover. Cook just to warm the potatoes and mussels, about 1 minute. Serve the chowder in deep bowls with the *fettunta*.

> TIP Prince Edward Island mussels have their beards (the cords that the mussels use to secure themselves to their growing location) removed before sale. Other varieties usually come to market with their beards intact. To remove the tough, inedible beards, just use a pair of pliers to pull them off.

VELVETY MUSHROOM SOUP

Vellutata di funghi misti

• •

Makes 6 to 8 servings

In Tuscany, fall is wild mushroom season, and virtually every man, woman, and child scours the countryside for porcini and other fungi for make into seasonal dishes like this velvety soup. There is a Tuscan saying, "If your future father-in-law offers to show you his secret porcini hunting grounds in the woods, he is going to let you marry his daughter . . . or he is going to murder you and bury your body under a tree." In the United States, fresh porcini are rare, so we use the various cultivated mushrooms that are available and flavor them with dried porcini.

1 ounce dried porcini
1 cup boiling water
2 tablespoons unsalted butter
2 teaspoons extra-virgin olive oil
⅓ cup sliced shallots
12 ounces sliced mixed fresh mushrooms, such as cremini, stemmed shiitake, and oyster

3 medium Yukon Gold potatoes, peeled and cut into ¾-inch dice (about 14 ounces)
½ cup freshly grated Parmigiano-Reggiano cheese, plus more for serving
Sea salt and freshly ground black pepper
Chopped fresh flat-leaf parsley, for serving

1. Soak the dried porcini in the boiling water in a small bowl until it softens, about 15 minutes. Lift the porcini out of the water, leaving any grit in the bowl, and coarsely chop it. Line a wire sieve with a moistened and squeezed out paper towel and set it over another bowl. Strain the liquid through the sieve to remove any grit. Set the soaked mushrooms and the strained liquid aside.

2. Heat the butter with the oil in a large saucepan over medium heat. Add the shallots and cook, stirring occasionally, until they turn golden, about 3 minutes. Stir in the mushrooms and cook, uncovered, until they begin to soften, about 5 minutes. Add the potatoes, cover, and cook until they begin to loose their raw look, about 3 minutes.

3. Add the soaked mushrooms with their liquid and 6 cups of cold water. Bring to a boil over high heat. Reduce the heat to medium low. Cover with the lid ajar and simmer, stirring occasionally, until the potatoes are very tender, about 25 minutes. Remove from the heat and stir in the Parmigiano.

4. Using an immersion blender, puree the soup in the saucepan until it is smooth. (Or let the soup cool and puree it in batches in a blender with the lid ajar, and reheat before serving.) Season to taste with the salt and pepper. Serve hot, in soup bowls, sprinkled with the parsley.

TIP If you use wild mushrooms, be sure to brush them clean. They are spongy and soak up liquid, so don't rinse them unless absolutely necessary.

CARROT AND GARBANZO BEAN SOUP

Minestra di carote e ceci

● ●

Makes 6 to 8 servings

This appetizingly orange soup is light but not too delicate. Because the carrots are front and center, make an effort to use freshly harvested, local, and preferably organic ones. The garbanzo bean mixture adds a visual and textural accent, and the fried rosemary is a nice, crispy garnish.

SOUP
1 small red onion, thinly sliced
2 tablespoons extra-virgin olive oil
2 pounds carrots
3 garlic cloves, crushed
One 3-inch sprig fresh rosemary
5 cups Vegetable Broth (page 67)
One 15-ounce can garbanzo beans
   (chickpeas), drained and rinsed
Sea salt and freshly ground black pepper

GARBANZO "SALAD"
1 tablespoon fresh lemon juice
1 tablespoon extra-virgin olive oil
1 teaspoon very finely chopped fresh rosemary
One 15-ounce can garbanzo beans
   (chickpeas), drained and rinsed
Sea salt and freshly ground black pepper

FRIED ROSEMARY
2 tablespoons extra-virgin olive oil
Two 3-inch sprigs fresh rosemary

1. To make the soup: Put the onion and oil in a large saucepan over medium-low heat and cook, stirring occasionally, until the onion is tender but not browned, about 5 minutes. Add the carrots, garlic, and rosemary and stir well. Cover and cook until the carrots begin to soften, about 5 minutes.

2. Add the broth and garbanzo beans and bring to a boil over high heat. Reduce the heat to low and cover with the lid ajar. Simmer until the carrots are very tender, about 30 minutes. Discard the rosemary sprig. Using an immersion blender, puree the soup in the saucepan until it is smooth. (Or let the soup cool, puree in batches in a blender with the lid ajar, and reheat before serving.) Season to taste with the salt and pepper.

3. To make the garbanzo "salad": Whisk the lemon juice, oil, and chopped rosemary in a medium bowl. Add the garbanzo beans and toss to combine. Season to taste with the salt and pepper. Set the mixture aside at room temperature.

4. To make the fried rosemary: Put the oil and rosemary in a small skillet over medium heat and cook, occasionally turning the sprigs, just until the rosemary leaves are crisp, about 3 minutes. Transfer the sprigs to paper towels to drain and cool and discard the oil. Remove the leaves from the stems and discard the stems.

5. To serve, spoon the soup into bowls. Add a spoonful of the room-temperature garbanzo "salad" into the center of each serving and sprinkle with the fried rosemary.

VEGETABLE BROTH

Brodo vegetale

• •

Makes about 4 cups

You might be surprised to see that we recommend vegetable broth instead of poultry or meat stock in our recipes, but it is versatile and complements meat, seafood, and poultry dishes. Plus, not that we are impatient people, but it takes less time to coax vegetables into broth than bones into stock. (And we usually have the vegetables in the fridge too.) This broth is left unsalted because the final dish will be seasoned.

1 large red onion, coarsely chopped

1 large carrot, coarsely chopped

1 large celery rib, coarsely chopped

1. Bring 6 cups of water, the onion, carrot, and celery to a boil in a large saucepan over high heat. Reduce the heat to medium low. Simmer, uncovered, until full flavored and reduced by about one-quarter, about 45 minutes.

2. Strain the broth in a wire sieve over a bowl, pressing hard on the solids. (The broth can be cooled, covered, and refrigerated for up to 3 days, or frozen for up to 3 months.)

LARGE BATCH VEGETABLE BROTH

Use 8 cups water, 2 medium red onions, 2 medium carrots, 2 medium celery ribs. Follow the Vegetable Broth instructions above for cooking and storing.

SALADS

BABY GREENS WITH GRAPEFRUIT AND MINT

Insalata mista al pompelmo e menta

● ●

Makes 4 to 6 servings

We always serve a salad with dinner, and the ever popular "mixed baby greens" is usually the main ingredient. But it can get repetitious. Here's an easy way that we found to mix things up. We raided the fruit bowl for the grapefruit, found some mint in the fridge . . . and the rest, as they say, is history. It is very often on the menu when we have company because it is totally unpretentious, but impressively flavorful.

2 grapefruits
1½ tablespoons red wine vinegar
⅓ cup plus 1 tablespoon extra-virgin olive oil

5 ounces mixed baby greens
2 tablespoons finely shredded fresh mint
Sea salt and freshly ground black pepper

1. Cut the top and bottom from the grapefruit so it stands securely on the work surface. Using a serrated knife, following the curve of the fruit, cut off the rind where the bitter pith meets the flesh. Trim away any bits of clinging pith. Working over a bowl, cut between the membranes to release the flesh in clean segments (in restaurant kitchens, these are called *supremes*), reserving any grapefruit juice. Repeat with the second grapefruit.

2. Strain 2 tablespoons of the grapefruit juice into a small bowl. Add the vinegar. Gradually whisk in the oil.

3. Toss the greens and vinaigrette in a large bowl. Serve on plates or in shallow bowls, topping each with grapefruit segments and a sprinkle of the mint. Season to taste with the salt and pepper. Serve immediately.

BEET AND PEAR CARPACCIO

Carpaccio di barbabietole e pere

• •

Makes 4 servings

G: *Here's a free art history lesson to go with a wonderful salad. The original version of carpaccio, paper-thin slices of beef drizzled with a pale mayonnaise, has been on the menu of Harry's Bar in Venice for almost fifty years. The dish is named for the Venetian painter, who sometimes juxtaposed red and white to dramatic effect. Nowadays, anything thinly sliced is dubbed carpaccio, although I bet the painter himself would recognize the magenta-red beets against the white pears as his particular style. A sprinkle of sharp Gorgonzola contrasts the sweet beets and pears.*

3 medium beets, greens discarded
2 tablespoons extra-virgin olive oil, plus more for rubbing on beets
2 ripe pears, such as Comice or Anjou
2 tablespoons fresh lemon juice
¼ teaspoon sea salt

¼ teaspoon freshly ground black pepper
3 ounces Gorgonzola dolce, crumbled (about ¾ cup)
3 tablespoons finely chopped walnuts, toasted (see Note)
4 teaspoons minced fresh mint

1. Position a rack in the center of the oven and preheat the oven to 400°F.

2. Scrub the beets under cold running water and pat them dry. Rub them lightly with the oil. Wrap each beet tightly in aluminum foil and place them on a baking sheet. Bake until the beets are tender when pierced with the tip of a sharp knife, about 1 hour 15 minutes, depending on their size. Unwrap the beets and let cool until warm. Slip off the skins. Cover and refrigerate the beets until chilled, at least 2 hours or up to 2 days.

3. Core the pears, but do not peel them. Cut lengthwise into very thin slices about 1/16 inch thick. Cut the beets crosswise into rounds about 1/16 inch thick.

4. Whisk the lemon juice, salt, and pepper in a small bowl. Gradually whisk in the remaining 2 tablespoons oil.

5. For each serving, using one-fourth of the beets and pears, scatter the slices on a dinner plate. Drizzle the lemon dressing over each, top with the Gorgonzola and a sprinkle of the walnuts and mint. Serve immediately.

NOTE To toast walnuts, spread the nuts out on a small rimmed baking sheet. Bake in a preheated oven at 350°F, stirring occasionally, until toasted, 10 to 15 minutes. Let cool completely before using.

SUMMER VEGETABLE SALAD
WITH CHERRY MOZZARELLA AND BASIL

Insalata estiva

••

Makes 4 to 6 servings

Every cook needs an easy summertime salad based on sweet and juicy tomatoes and aromatic basil to throw together at a moment's notice. When the weather is hot, we always have a bowl of beautiful tomatoes from the farmer's market, and there usually seems to be leftover grilled corn on the cob in the fridge. (We're providing instructions for broiled corn on the cob, just in case you don't have any handy.) Mozzarella ciliegine, *cherry-sized balls of cheese, are the perfect match for the tomatoes. This is best served soon after making so the tomato juices don't get a chance to water down the salad.*

2 ears corn, husked
1 pint heirloom cherry tomatoes, cut in halves
6 ounces drained cherry mozzarella balls
    (*ciliegine*), cut in halves
⅓ cup finely chopped red onion

2 tablespoons coarsely chopped fresh basil,
    plus more for serving
1½ tablespoons balsamic vinegar
⅓ cup extra-virgin olive oil
Sea salt and freshly ground black pepper

1. Position the broiler rack about 6 inches from the source of heat and preheat the broiler on high.

2. Place the corn directly on the rack and broil, turning occasionally, until the kernels are tinged with browned spots, about 10 minutes. Let the corn cool. To remove the kernels, stand an ear vertically on its wide end. Holding it steady, starting at the top of the ear, use a knife to cut off the kernels where they meet the cob. You should have about 1 cup kernels, depending on the size of the ears.

3. Toss the corn kernels, cherry tomatoes, mozzarella, red onion, and basil in a large bowl. Drizzle with the vinegar and oil and toss again. Season to taste with the salt and pepper. Top with the additional basil and serve immediately.

FENNEL AND APPLE SLAW

Insalata di mele e finocchi

• •

Makes 6 servings

Shredded vegetable salad (aka slaw) is not very well known in Italy. The first time Gabriele had Southern-style pulled pork, it was served with coleslaw, and he immediately saw how it could go with Italian roast pork too. So here is a Tuscan slaw, with fennel and shredded apple to make a light and brightly flavored salad. Make this to serve with grilled chicken or pork or sandwiches of any kind. We don't have to tell you that it is a great picnic dish and would be very good alongside the Tuscan Fried Chicken (page 189).

1 large lemon
1 large fennel (anise) bulb
2 Granny Smith apples
1 tablespoon white wine vinegar
1 teaspoon honey

⅛ teaspoon hot red pepper flakes
2 tablespoons finely chopped fresh cilantro or
   flat-leaf parsley
Sea salt and freshly ground black pepper

1. Cut the lemon in half and squeeze to measure 2 tablespoons of the juice. Transfer the squeezed lemon halves and any remaining lemon juice to a medium bowl and add about 4 cups of iced water.

2. Trim off the stalks, fronds, and tough outer layer from the fennel. Trim the bottom of the bulb. Cut the bulb in half lengthwise. With the tip of a small sharp knife, dig out the solid core from the bottom of the bulb. Discard the trimmings. Using a V-slicer or mandoline, cut the fennel into thin slices. Transfer the slices to the lemon water. Let stand to crisp for 15 to 20 minutes.

3. Using the large holes on a box grater, press hard to shred the unpeeled apples down to the core, discarding the core and tough bits of skin. Drain the fennel well, discarding the ice, and dry the fennel by patting it with paper towels or in a salad spinner.

4. Whisk the reserved lemon juice, vinegar, honey, and red pepper flakes in a medium bowl. Add the fennel, apples with any juices, and the cilantro and mix well, seasoning to taste with the salt and black pepper. Cover and refrigerate to blend the flavors for at least 1 hour. (The slaw can be refrigerated for up to 1 day.) Let the slaw stand at room temperature for 15 minutes before serving.

TIP Some people can't stand cilantro. This phenomenon seems to be genetic and
not just personal. In that case, just leave it out. When growing up, Gabriele saw
cilantro (*coriandolo*) in some markets, but his family never cooked with it. He had
to get to LA to really appreciate the herb. If you wish, substitute flat-leaf parsley or,
if you like the mild licorice flavor of fennel, use the finely chopped fennel fronds.

FARRO SALAD WITH BUTTERNUT SQUASH AND HERBS

Insalata invernale di farro

. . . .

Wine Pairing: Pinot Bianco

Makes 6 servings

We serve this at the restaurant on the side with soups. It is also fantastic with all kinds of roasts, especially chicken and pork. If you buy farro in a package, follow the directions for the cooking time, as they vary widely. Just be flexible with the cooking time and do not sweat it . . . after all, this is served at room temp and you will be making it ahead, anyway. Above all, it is a nice healthy change from potatoes or rice.

1 tablespoon extra-virgin olive oil, plus more for oiling and serving
2 cups (½-inch) diced butternut squash
One 3-inch sprig fresh rosemary
Two 3-inch sprigs fresh thyme
Sea salt and freshly ground black pepper

1½ cups semi-pearled farro
2 tablespoons finely chopped fresh flat-leaf parsley
2 ounces well-crumbled ricotta salata (about ½ cup)

1. Position a rack in the center of the oven and preheat the oven to 400°F. Lightly oil a half-sheet pan.

2. Toss the butternut squash with the oil, rosemary, and thyme on the prepared baking sheet. Season to taste with the salt and pepper. Bake, stirring occasionally, until the squash is roasted and tender, 20 to 30 minutes. Let cool.

3. Bring a large pot of salted water to a boil over high heat. Stir in the farro and return to a boil. Adjust the heat to medium and boil until the farro is tender, about 20 minutes. (Or longer for whole grain farro, up to 45 minutes.) Drain and rinse under cold running water. Drain well. Let cool.

4. Crumble the rosemary and thyme leaves off their stems onto the butternut squash and discard the stems. Mix the squash, farro, and parsley in a medium bowl. Mix in all but 2 tablespoons of the ricotta salata. Season to taste with the salt and pepper. Drizzle with olive oil, sprinkle with the reserved ricotta salata, and serve at room temperature.

MARINATED LENTILS AND BURRATA

Insalata di lenticchie e burrata

• •

Wine Pairing: Prosecco or Pinot Grigio

Makes 4 servings

We have great memories of al fresco meals, both in the Tuscan countryside and in our Brooklyn back-yard. But this particular combination of simple lentils and creamy burrata is the perfect example of how Tuscans can take humble foods and turn them into something extraordinary. There's nothing complicated about this marinated salad, and its "secret," if there is one, is to let the ingredients speak for themselves.

LENTILS
1 tablespoon extra-virgin olive oil
1 small red onion, finely chopped
1 medium carrot, cut into ¼-inch dice
1 medium celery rib, cut into ¼-inch dice
2 garlic cloves, minced
1 cup green lentils (*lentilles du Puy*, see Note),
    rinsed and drained
½ teaspoon sea salt

LEMON-PARSLEY DRESSING
2 tablespoons fresh lemon juice
⅛ teaspoon hot red pepper flakes
Sea salt and freshly ground black pepper
¼ cup extra-virgin olive oil
2 tablespoons minced fresh flat-leaf parsley

8 large basil leaves, torn into small pieces
2 burrata cheeses (about 14 ounces total)

1. To make the lentils: Heat the oil in a medium saucepan over medium heat. Add the onion, carrot, and celery and cook, stirring occasionally, until the vegetables soften, about 5 minutes. Stir in the garlic and cook until fragrant, about 1 minute. Stir in the lentils and add enough water to cover the lentils by 1 inch. Bring to a boil over high heat. Stir in the salt. Reduce the heat to medium and cook at a steady simmer until the lentils are barely tender (not mushy or falling apart), about 20 minutes. Drain well in a wire sieve. Transfer to a medium serving bowl and let cool.

2. To make the dressing: Whisk the lemon juice, red pepper flakes, a pinch of salt, and a few grinds of black pepper together in a small bowl. Gradually whisk in the oil. Whisk in the parsley. Pour over the lentils and mix gently. Season to taste with the salt and pepper. (The salad can be covered and refrigerated for up to 8 hours. Reseason the chilled salad before serving.)

3. Mix in most of the basil. Tear each burrata into quarters and place on the salad. Sprinkle with the remaining basil and serve.

NOTE While you can make this with standard brown lentils, it is worth search-ing out the small dark-green ones, often imported from France. (Between us, they are not Italian, but we like them anyway!) If using large brown lentils, increase the cooking time to about 30 minutes.

GREEK QUINOA SALAD

Insalata greca di quinoa

● ●

Makes 6 servings

G: *I never thought about using grains in a salad until I started cooking in American kitchens. When I first had quinoa, which comes from Latin America, I immediately started making it with Mediterranean flavors. This Greek-inspired salad stands on its own as a lunch or picnic salad; I like to serve it as a side dish to grilled fish. Don't be surprised to see feta cheese in this dish, because Italians cook with it too. After all, Greece isn't very far away from Tuscany!*

¾ cup quinoa, any color
1½ teaspoons sea salt, plus more for seasoning
2 Israeli (or Persian) cucumbers, unpeeled, scrubbed, and cut into ½-inch dice
1 cup halved cherry tomatoes, preferably heirlooms of mixed colors
⅓ cup pitted and chopped oil-cured olives

2 scallions, white and green parts, finely chopped
1 tablespoon finely chopped fresh dill
2 teaspoons finely chopped fresh mint
½ cup crumbled feta cheese
2 tablespoons fresh lemon juice
Freshly ground black pepper
½ cup extra-virgin olive oil

1. Put the quinoa in a fine wire sieve and rinse well to remove its invisible coating. (If you don't do this, the quinoa will be bitter.) Transfer to a medium saucepan and add 2¼ cups water and ½ teaspoon salt. Bring to a boil over high heat. Reduce the heat to low and tightly cover the saucepan. Simmer until the quinoa is tender and has absorbed the liquid, about 20 minutes. Using a fork, fluff the quinoa and transfer it to a medium bowl. Let the quinoa cool completely.

2. Meanwhile, toss the cucumbers with 1 teaspoon salt. Let them stand in a wired sieve in the sink for 30 minutes. Rinse well and pat dry with paper towels.

3. Toss the quinoa, cucumbers, tomatoes, olives, scallions, dill, mint, and feta cheese in a large bowl. Whisk the lemon juice with a pinch each of salt and pepper in a small bowl. Gradually whisk in the oil. Drizzle over the quinoa mixture and toss again. Season to taste with the salt and pepper. (The salad can be covered and refrigerated for up to 8 hours.) Serve chilled or at room temperature.

CHILLED ASPARAGUS WITH TARRAGON VINAIGRETTE AND MIMOSA EGGS

Insalata di asparagi e uova

• • • • • • • • • • • • • • • • • • • •

Makes 4 to 6 servings

We like the versatility of this salad. Of course, you can serve it any time, but the eggs make it especially nice as a brunch dish. The components of this salad can be made ahead and pulled together for serving at the last minute. The spears are tossed with a lemony dressing, then finished with a shower of grated hard-boiled eggs. The tiny egg flakes are called mimosa *because the yellow and white color combination is reminiscent of small mimosa flowers.*

2 large eggs	Sea salt and freshly ground black pepper
2 pounds asparagus, woody stems discarded	½ cup extra-virgin olive oil
2 tablespoons fresh lemon juice	2 teaspoons finely chopped fresh tarragon

1. Place the eggs in a small saucepan and add enough cold water to cover. Bring just to a boil over medium heat. Remove from the heat and tightly cover the saucepan. Let the eggs stand for 12 minutes. Carefully drain the eggs and transfer to a bowl of iced water. Let stand until chilled, about 10 minutes. Shell the eggs. Cover and refrigerate until ready to serve, up to 1 day.

2. Bring a large pot of salted water to a boil over high heat. Add the asparagus and cook until crisp-tender, about 5 minutes. Drain, rinse under cold running water, and bring to room temperature. Pat the asparagus dry with paper towels. Wrap the asparagus in dry paper towels, put in a zippered plastic bag, and refrigerate until chilled, at least 1 hour or up to 1 day.

3. Whisk the lemon juice, ¼ teaspoon salt, and ¼ teaspoon pepper in a small bowl. Gradually whisk in the oil. (The vinaigrette can be stored at room temperature for up to 8 hours.)

4. Stir the tarragon into the lemon vinaigrette. Toss the asparagus and the vinaigrette in a large bowl, keeping the asparagus intact. Arrange the asparagus on a large platter and drizzle with any leftover vinaigrette in the bowl. Using the medium holes on a box grater, grate the hard-boiled eggs, using both the whites and the yolks, over the asparagus, letting the eggs fall loosely and mound on the spears. Season the eggs with salt and pepper and serve.

SHRIMP, FIG, AND MELON SALAD

Insalata di scampi, fichi e melone

••

Wine Pairing: Verdicchio or Vermentino
Makes 4 servings

Whenever we serve this salad, we are reminded of the kind of lunch that takes place under a sun-dappled pergola in late summer, when melons are at their peak and figs are just coming in. In Fiesole, we use a local melon (similar to a cantaloupe with darker stripes and flesh) and figs from Dalmatia (sporting purple-black skins and deep red flesh). You can make this with whatever melon and figs you have handy as long as they are very ripe and sweet. Large shrimp make the most visual impact, but use whatever size your budget allows. You will need a melon baller to prepare the melon.

LEMON DRESSING
2 tablespoons fresh lemon juice
¼ cup extra-virgin olive oil
Sea salt and freshly ground black pepper

1 tablespoon extra-virgin olive oil
2 garlic cloves, coarsely chopped
¼ cup dry white wine, such as Pinot Grigio

SCAMPI
¼ teaspoon sea salt
Pinch of cayenne pepper
12 colossal (U-15 count) shrimp, peeled and
  deveined

1 ripe melon, such as Tuscan or cantaloupe,
  halved and seeded
3 ounces arugula (about 3 packed cups)
6 dark-skinned figs, such as Black Mission, each
  cut lengthwise into thin slices

1. To make the dressing: Pour the lemon juice into a small bowl. Gradually whisk in the oil. Season to taste with the salt and black pepper.

2. To cook the scampi: Mix the salt and cayenne pepper, and season the shrimp with the salt mixture. Heat the oil and garlic cloves in a large skillet over medium-high heat, stirring often, just until the garlic is golden, about 1 minute. Add the shrimp to the skillet and cook, turning occasionally, just until the shrimp begins to turn pink, about 2 minutes. Add the wine and cook until the shrimp is opaque and the wine is almost evaporated, about 2 minutes more. Transfer the shrimp to a plate and let it cool.

3. Using a melon baller, scoop out balls from the melon. Toss the arugula and melon balls in a medium bowl.

4. For each salad, arrange one-quarter of the sliced figs in a wide circle on a dinner plate. Fill in the empty center of the fig circle with one-quarter of the arugula salad mixture, and top with 3 of the shrimp, intertwining the tails so the shrimp stand up. Drizzle the dressing evenly over each salad and serve.

CRAB AND AVOCADO SALAD

Insalata di granchio e avocado

· ·

Wine Pairing: Prosecco
Makes 2 servings

D: *This is an easy salad to make for lunch or as a supper during the warm weather when you just don't feel like heating up the stove. I mention summer heat because the first time we had this was during peekytoe crab season in Maine. If you want to use another crab variety, say the Dungeness from the West Coast, the season might be in the winter. The important thing is to make it with fresh crab—it just isn't as good with the canned pasteurized version. This is a recipe for a sexy meal for two—but you can always increase the amounts for more people.*

8 ounces fresh crabmeat, preferably peekytoe,
    picked over for shells and cartilage
Finely grated zest of ½ lemon
2 tablespoons fresh lemon juice
1 tablespoon minced red onion
1 tablespoon extra-virgin olive oil
1 tablespoon finely chopped fresh flat-leaf
    parsley

1 tablespoon finely chopped fresh basil
½ jalapeño, seeds removed and sliced paper-
    thin
1 ripe avocado, cut into ¾-inch dice
Sea salt and freshly ground pepper
4 large leaves butter lettuce

1. Mix the crabmeat, lemon zest and juice, onion, oil, parsley, basil, and jalapeño in a medium bowl to combine. Add the avocado and toss very gently to combine, keeping the avocado intact. Season to taste with the salt and pepper. (The salad can be covered and refrigerated for up to 2 hours.)

2. For each serving, place 2 lettuce leaves on a dinner plate and top with half of the salad. Serve immediately.

BREAKFAST

EGGS IN TOMATO SAUCE

Uova al pomodoro

• •

Makes 4 servings

G: *This recipe brings me right back to cold mornings on the farm when we needed something to warm us up. That's when my father would take some leftover tomato sauce from dinner and use it to make these eggs over a fire in the fireplace. (We've provided a from-scratch recipe for tomato sauce in case you don't have three cups or so of leftover sauce lying around.) We like to serve this as a late breakfast with plenty of Tuscan Country Toast (page 59). If you happen to have a few cups of leftover red sauce, the meal comes together in no time. You can also make it in mini cast-iron cocottes, with one ramekin for each burner on your stove. In that case, use about ½ cup of sauce and one egg per ramekin.*

2 tablespoons extra-virgin olive oil
2 garlic cloves, crushed
One 28-ounce can tomatoes in juice, pureed in a blender
Pinch of hot red pepper flakes

Sea salt and freshly ground black pepper
8 large eggs, preferably organic
2 teaspoons finely chopped fresh flat-leaf parsley
Tuscan Country Toast (page 59), without garlic, for serving

1. Heat the oil and garlic together in a large, wide skillet over medium heat until the garlic is fragrant and softened, about 2 minutes. Use a slotted spoon to discard the garlic. Stir in the tomatoes and red pepper flakes and bring to a simmer. Reduce the heat to low and simmer, stirring often, until very slightly reduced, about 20 minutes. Season the sauce to taste with the salt and black pepper.

2. Crack each egg directly above the sauce, moving around the skillet to space the eggs evenly apart. Season the eggs to taste with the salt and pepper. Cover the skillet and cook just until the whites set, 3 to 5 minutes.

3. Using a large spoon, transfer the eggs and sauce to wide bowls, trying to keep the eggs intact. Sprinkle with the parsley and serve hot with the *fettunta*.

BAKED EGGS IN CUPS WITH POLENTA AND MUSHROOMS

Uova in tazza con polenta e funghi

• •

Makes 4 servings

G: *We had a Sunday morning ritual at the farm in Fiesole. My early-rising grandfather, Renato, would start a fire in the fireplace and by the time everyone was up, it had died down to coals to use for cooking. These eggs cooked with polenta and mushrooms were my favorite "brunch." We always used the same ancient coffee mugs for this dish. It was my job to break the egg into each mug—I was so proud to be the one responsible for topping our meal with its main ingredient. Renato would then literally screw each cup into the deep bed of coals, cover them with a flat piece of wood, and the heat would cook them quickly. These days, we use an oven, but the memories of the fireplace meal remain.*

D: *We use splatterware metal coffee mugs when we make these in Brooklyn. You can also use the mini cocottes or the large Pyrex custard cups sold at most supermarkets. Whatever you choose, just be sure it is ovenproof.*

Special equipment: 4 large (about 1½ cups capacity) ovenproof coffee mugs or ramekins

MUSHROOMS
1 tablespoon extra-virgin olive oil
½ cup (¼-inch) diced guanciale or pancetta
3 portobello mushrooms, cut into ½-inch dice
3 garlic cloves, crushed
Two 3-inch sprigs fresh thyme
One 3-inch sprig fresh mint
Two 3-inch sprigs *nipitella* or 1 additional sprig
    fresh mint
Sea salt and freshly ground black pepper

POLENTA
1 tablespoon unsalted butter
½ teaspoon sea salt
¾ cup instant polenta

Extra-virgin olive oil, for oiling the mugs
4 large eggs
Sea salt and freshly ground black pepper
2 tablespoons freshly grated Pecorino Romano

1. Position a rack in the center of the oven and preheat the oven to 350°F.

2. To make the mushrooms: Heat the oil in a large nonstick skillet over medium-high heat. Add the guanciale and cook, stirring occasionally, until browned, about 4 minutes. Add the mushrooms, garlic cloves, thyme, mint, and *nipitella*. Season to taste with the salt and pepper. Cook, stirring occasionally, until they release their liquid, about 5 minutes. Remove and discard the garlic and herbs.

3. To make the polenta: Bring 2½ cups water, butter, and salt to a boil in a medium saucepan over high heat. Reduce the heat to low and gradually stir in the polenta. Cook just until the polenta begins to thicken, about 1 minute. Remove from the heat—the polenta should only be lightly thickened; it will firm up during baking.

4. Lightly oil the four coffee mugs. Spoon half of the mushroom mixture among the mugs. Top each with equal amounts of the polenta, followed by the remaining mushrooms. Break an egg into each mug and lightly season with the salt and pepper. Sprinkle with the Pecorino.

5. Place the mugs on a large rimmed baking sheet. Top them with a second baking sheet or a sheet of aluminum foil. Bake until the whites are set but the yolks are still runny, about 10 minutes. Remove from the oven. Let the mugs stand for a few minutes and serve hot.

ASPARAGUS AND PROSCIUTTO TORTINO

Tortino di asparagi e prosciutto

• •

Wine Pairing: Prosecco
Makes 6 to 8 servings

A tortino is a quiche with an Italian accent. Like its French cousin, it is a popular long-standing brunch dish, with the menu rounded out by a green salad (perhaps the Baby Greens with Grapefruit and Mint on page 71) and a cold flute of prosecco. We've made many different ones over the years and this is a particular favorite. In spring, during our short local asparagus season, we rush down to the Grand Army Plaza farmer's market to buy as much as we can for dishes like this one. The eggs, cheese, and pastry make a perfect showcase for the fresh flavor of the asparagus. To reduce the work in the morning, we've given make-ahead instructions for the crust and filling to get them out of the way the night before. That just leaves mixing the custard up and baking.

Special equipment: 9-inch tart pan with removable bottom

DOUGH
- 1¼ cups (175 grams) unbleached all-purpose flour, plus more for dusting
- ¼ teaspoon sea salt
- 4 ounces (1 stick) cold unsalted butter, cut into ½-inch cubes
- ¼ cup iced water, plus more as needed

FILLING
- 8 ounces thin asparagus, woody stems discarded
- 1 tablespoon extra-virgin olive oil
- ¼ cup (¼-inch) diced prosciutto
- 2 tablespoons minced shallot
- 1 cup (4 ounces) shredded fontina cheese, preferably Fontina Val d'Aosta
- 2 large eggs
- ¼ teaspoon sea salt
- ¼ teaspoon freshly ground black pepper
- Few gratings fresh nutmeg
- 1 cup whole milk

1. To make the dough: Stir the flour and salt in a medium bowl. Add the butter. Using a pastry blender or two knives, cut the butter into the mixture until it resembles coarse crumbs with some pea-sized pieces of butter. Gradually stir in enough of the iced water until the mixture is thoroughly moistened. It may look dry, but should hold together when a handful is pressed in your fist. If necessary, sprinkle in additional iced water, a teaspoon at a time to get the correct consistency. Gather up the dough and shape into a thick disk. Wrap in plastic wrap and refrigerate until chilled but not hard, 45 minutes to 1 hour.

2. Position a rack in the lower third of the oven and preheat the oven to 375°F.

3. Lightly dust the work surface with flour. (If you wish, draw a 12-inch-diameter circle in the flour to use as a template to get the correct size for the dough.) Unwrap the dough and dust the top with flour too. Roll out the dough into a round about 12 inches in diameter and ⅛ inch thick. Transfer the dough to the tart pan, fitting the dough into the corners without stretching it. Roll the rolling pin over the pan to cut off the excess dough; discard the trimmings. Freeze the dough-lined pan for about 15 minutes.

4. Line the dough-lined pan with aluminum foil and top with pie weights or dried beans. Place on a baking sheet and bake until the exposed dough around the edges looks set and dry, about 15 minutes. Lift up and remove the foil with the weights. Continue baking until the crust is just beginning to brown, about 10 minutes more. Remove the pan from the oven. (The crust can be cooled, covered with plastic wrap, and stored at room temperature for up to 18 hours. Warm in a preheated 375°F oven for 5 minutes before using.)

5. To make the filling: Cut the tips off the asparagus and set them aside. Cut the spears crosswise into ½-inch pieces and add to the tips. Heat the oil in a medium saucepan over medium heat. Add the prosciutto and cook, stirring occasionally, until it is lightly browned, about 3 minutes. Add the shallot and stir occasionally until it softens, about 1 minute. Stir in the asparagus and ¼ cup water. Cover with the lid ajar and cook until the water is evaporated and the asparagus is tender, about 5 minutes. Remove from the heat. (The asparagus mixture can be cooled, covered, and refrigerated for up to 18 hours. Let stand at room temperature for 1 hour before using.)

6. Sprinkle the fontina evenly over the crust in the pan, followed by the cooled asparagus mixture. Whisk the eggs, salt, pepper, and nutmeg in a medium bowl, and whisk in the milk. Pour the custard over the filling.

7. Bake for 10 minutes at 375°F. Reduce the heat to 350°F and continue baking until the filling is evenly puffed and lightly browned, about 30 minutes. Let cool in the pan for 10 minutes. Remove the pan sides and serve warm or cooled to room temperature.

CRANBERRY POLENTA COFFEE CAKE

Torta di mirtilli rossi

• •

Makes 8 servings

As far as we are concerned, this is a fairly perfect coffee cake. It's easy to make, especially if you have an electric mixer to whip the egg mixture. It is a good recipe to have in rotation during the winter holidays, when cranberries are in season and we seem to have a lot of houseguests encouraging us to linger around the breakfast table. In Italy, we make it with blueberries standing in for the all-American cranberries.

¾ cup extra-virgin olive oil, plus more for the pan
1 cup (140 grams) unbleached all-purpose flour, plus more for dusting the pan
½ cup yellow cornmeal, preferably stone-ground
2 teaspoons baking powder
½ teaspoon sea salt
¾ cup sugar

3 large eggs, at room temperature (see Tip)
Finely grated zest of 1 orange
¼ cup whole milk
Seeds scraped from 1 vanilla bean or 1 teaspoon vanilla extract
1 cup fresh or frozen cranberries
Confectioners' sugar, for serving

1. Position a rack in the center of the oven and preheat the oven to 350°F. Lightly brush a 10-inch fluted tube pan with oil. Dust the inside of the pan with flour and tap out the excess flour.

2. Whisk the flour, cornmeal, baking powder, and salt together in a medium bowl. Whip the sugar, eggs, and orange zest in a stand mixer with the whisk attachment on medium-high speed to combine. Gradually beat in the oil. Continue whipping until the mixture is thick and pale, about 3 minutes. (If you using an electric hand mixer, allow 4 minutes.) Reduce the mixer speed to low. Add the flour mixture and mix until smooth. Add the milk and vanilla and mix until combined. Using a rubber spatula, fold in the cranberries. Scrape the mixture into the prepared pan and smooth the top.

3. Bake until the cake is golden brown and springs back when gently pressed with your fingertips, about 50 minutes. Let cool in the pan on a wire cake rack for 10 minutes. Run a knife around the edge of the pan and down the entire tube to loosen the cake. Invert the pan to unmold the cake onto the rack and cool completely. Sift the confectioners' sugar over the top, slice, and serve.

TIP If you have forgotten to take the eggs out of the refrigerator, here is an easy fix. Put the uncracked eggs in a small bowl and cover them with hot tap water. Let the eggs stand for 5 minutes to lose their chill, drain them, and proceed with the recipe.

PANCETTA SCONES

Scones di pancetta

• •

Makes 6 scones

G: *This perfect breakfast snack was created for our customers, who are always looking for a morning treat to eat on the run. Freeze any leftovers to split and reheat in a toaster oven.*

D: *I'm a fan of this scone because I will always choose savory over sweet, especially at breakfast. Sometimes we'll make these bite-sized and serve them as antipasti with prosecco.*

1 scant cup (¼-inch) diced pancetta

2 cups (280 grams) unbleached all-purpose flour

½ cup plus 1 tablespoon freshly grated Parmigiano-Reggiano cheese

2 tablespoons sugar

1½ teaspoons baking powder

½ teaspoon baking soda

½ teaspoon sea salt

½ teaspoon freshly ground black pepper

4 ounces (1 stick) cold unsalted butter, cut into ½-inch cubes

⅓ cup whole milk, plus more for brushing

⅓ cup mascarpone cheese

1. Cook the pancetta in a medium skillet over medium heat, stirring occasionally, until crisp and browned, 6 to 8 minutes. Using a slotted spoon, transfer the pancetta to a paper-towel-lined plate to cool. Reserve 2 tablespoons of the rendered fat and discard the remainder.

2. Position a rack in the center of the oven and preheat the oven to 400°F. Line a large rimmed baking sheet with parchment paper or a silicone baking mat.

3. Whisk the flour, ½ cup of the Parmigiano, sugar, baking powder, baking soda, salt, and pepper together in a medium bowl. Add the butter and stir to coat with the flour mixture. Using a pastry blender or two knives, cut the butter into the mixture until it resembles coarse crumbs with some pea-sized pieces of butter. (You can also whisk all of the dry ingredients in the bowl of a standing electric mixer fitted with the paddle attachment. Add the butter and cut it in with the mixer on medium speed, about 2 minutes. Do not over mix.) Mix in the cooled pancetta.

4. Whisk the milk, mascarpone, and reserved fat in a small bowl. Pour into the flour mixture and stir (or mix on low speed) just until combined. Gather up the dough in the bowl into a ball.

5. Transfer the dough to the prepared baking sheet and pat it into a round about 8 inches wide and ¾ inch thick. Brush the top of the dough with the milk and sprinkle with the remaining tablespoon of Parmigiano. Using a large sharp knife for a clean slice, cut the round into six equal triangles. Separate the scones, leaving them about 1 inch apart.

6. Bake until the scones are golden brown, 20 to 25 minutes. Let cool until they are warm or serve at room temperature.

LEMON ROSEMARY MUFFINS

Muffins al rosmarino e limone

• •

Makes 10 muffins

G: *We make this sweet-and-savory muffin every day at our café. This is one recipe where we use dried herbs, as the flavor and texture of fresh rosemary varies a lot. The icing is completely optional, but it does give a nice (if sweet) finish to the muffins. Try this tender and aromatic muffin with a hot cup of tea.*

D: *One bite of this muffin and I am reminded of our garden in Italy with its lemons and rosemary. I think of it as a feminine muffin, very fragrant and pretty.*

MUFFINS

2¼ cups (315 grams) unbleached all-purpose flour
2 teaspoons crumbled dried rosemary
1 teaspoon sea salt
½ teaspoon baking powder
½ teaspoon baking soda
3 large eggs, at room temperature (see Tip, page 97)
⅔ cup sugar
6 ounces (1½ sticks) unsalted butter, melted and cooled to tepid

Freshly grated zest of 1 lemon
1 teaspoon fresh lemon juice
¾ teaspoon vanilla extract
⅔ cup sour cream

LEMON ICING

1 cup confectioners' sugar
2 tablespoons fresh lemon juice, as needed

1. Position a rack in the center of the oven and preheat the oven to 375°F. Line 10 muffin cups in a muffin pan with paper liners.

2. To make the muffins: Whisk the flour, rosemary, salt, baking powder, and baking soda together in a medium bowl. Whip the eggs in a medium bowl with an electric mixer set on high speed. Gradually beat in the sugar and whip until the mixture is pale yellow and almost tripled in volume, about 3 minutes. Gradually beat in the melted butter. Mix in the lemon zest, lemon juice, and vanilla. If using a standing mixer, change to the paddle attachment. On low speed, in thirds, add the flour mixture, alternating with two equal additions of the sour cream, mixing just until combined.

3. Divide the batter evenly among the muffin cups. Bake until the muffins are golden brown and spring back when the tops are gently pressed with a fingertip, 20 to 25 minutes. Let cool in the pan for 5 minutes. Remove from the pan and let cool completely.

4. To make the icing: Sift the confectioners' sugar into a small bowl. Stir in enough of the lemon juice to make a thick but pourable icing. Spoon the icing over the muffins. Let the icing set completely, about 30 minutes, and serve.

PANCAKES WITH MIXED BERRY–HONEY SAUCE

Pancakes con salsa ai frutti di bosco

• •

Makes 4 to 6 servings

D: *Whenever we visit Gabriele's family, I make them an American breakfast. However, it is impossible to find some of the necessary ingredients in Italian supermarkets, so I have to transport baking powder and baking soda. Of course, buttermilk doesn't travel so easily, so I make a substitute from yogurt and milk that works well. When I haven't imported maple syrup from the States, I mix up a great berry-honey sauce that gives the syrup a run for its money.*

G: *If you like to make pancakes, invest in a stovetop griddle. They are inexpensive and they give you much more cooking surface than a skillet. Since pancakes are only good when they are piping hot, being able to cook more than a couple at a time is a benefit for all parties. Lacking a griddle, heat up two skillets to make the job go more quickly.*

SAUCE
12 ounces strawberries, thinly sliced (about 2 cups)
One 6-ounce container raspberries (about 1⅓ cups)
½ cup honey

PANCAKES
2 cups (280 grams) unbleached all-purpose flour
2 tablespoons sugar
1½ teaspoons baking powder
1 teaspoon baking soda

½ teaspoon sea salt
1½ cups whole milk
1 cup plain low-fat or whole milk yogurt (not Greek-style)
2 ounces (½ stick) unsalted butter, melted and cooled to tepid
3 large eggs, separated, at room temperature
Canola oil, for oiling skillets (see Tip)
Softened unsalted butter, for serving

1. To make the sauce: Bring the strawberries, raspberries, and honey to a simmer, stirring occasionally. Remove from the heat and cover to keep warm.

2. Position racks in the center and bottom third of the oven and preheat the oven to 200°F.

3. To make the pancakes: Sift the flour, sugar, baking powder, baking soda, and salt together in a large bowl. Whisk the milk, yogurt, melted butter, and egg yolks together in another bowl. Whip the egg whites in a third bowl with an electric mixer or whisk until soft peaks form. Pour the milk mixture into the flour mixture and stir just until smooth—it can show a few small lumps. Fold the whites into the batter.

4. Heat 2 large skillets or a large griddle over medium-high heat. Flick some water from your finger-tips onto the skillets—the water should immediately form skittering balls. Lightly oil the skillets. Reduce the heat to medium. Using about ¼ cup of batter for each pancake, pour the batter onto the skillets. Cook until small holes appear all over the surface of the pancakes, about 1½ minutes. Flip the pancakes and continue cooking to brown the other side, about 1 minute more. Transfer the pancakes directly to the oven rack (do not use a baking sheet because you want the warm air to circulate around the pancakes to keep them from getting soggy). Repeat with the remaining batter.

5. Serve the pancakes warm with the butter and sauce on the side.

TIP An oil with a neutral flavor, such as canola, is the best choice for greasing the skillets for pancakes. Butter will burn . . . trust us! And olive oil is not the right flavor for pancakes. Trust us on that one too.

RASPBERRY AND ROSEMARY PRESERVES

Confettura di lamponi e rosmarino

•••

Makes about 2 pints

G: *My mother taught me how to make fruit preserves with this simple formula: Cook the fruit with half its weight of sugar and some lemon until it is thick enough to hold its shape on a cold plate. I suppose there are other recipes, but the great thing about this one is its versatility. I've used it for figs, plums, and all kinds of berries. The lemon is used as a natural pectin to help the preserves set.*

D: *Our recipe makes a small batch perfect to store in the fridge, plus it does not need to be hot-packed. We usually make a jar or two for our family, and a couple of jars for gifting. It doesn't have to be a holiday to give a friend a jar of homemade preserves!*

Special equipment: Four ½-pint glass canning jars with lids

2 pounds raspberries	2 tablespoons fresh lemon juice
2¼ cups sugar	Two 3-inch sprigs fresh rosemary
Zest strips from 1 lemon, removed with a vegetable peeler	

1. Place a saucer in the freezer to chill while making the preserves. It will be used to quickly chill the preserves and check them for consistency.

2. Combine the raspberries, sugar, lemon zest, lemon juice, and rosemary in a large, nonreactive, heavy-bottomed saucepan or enameled Dutch oven. Bring to a boil over high heat, stirring often, making sure that the sugar dissolves.

3. Reduce the heat to medium low. Simmer, stirring often to avoid scorching, until the mixture has thickened and reduced by about one-quarter, 45 minutes to 1 hour. To check for doneness, drop about 1 teaspoon of the preserves onto the chilled plate. Return to the freezer for 1 minute. If the preserves hold their shape in a jiggly mound on the plate, they are done.

4. Run the jars through the dishwasher and use them while they are hot. Or heat them in a saucepan of boiling water to cover for 5 minutes. Use tongs to remove the jars from the water and drain them, upside down, on a wire cake rack set over a kitchen towel. Dry them with another (very clean) kitchen towel. Soak the canning lids, but not the rings, in a bowl of hot tap water. Using a canning funnel or a large spoon, transfer the hot preserves to the hot jars, wiping away any excess preserves on the rims with a hot, wet towel. Drain the lids and use with the rings to cover the jars. Let stand until cooled. (The preserves can be refrigerated for up to 2 months.)

OUR COOKBOOKS

D: When guests come to our house, they might reasonably think that we are all going to sit down in our living room or parlor. We would . . . except we don't have a sofa. The space that would normally be taken up by a sofa and chairs has been filled with stacks of cookbooks on the floor.

Everyone migrates to the kitchen table and we hang out there. The living room is one of the smaller rooms in the house, anyway. It's not that we don't appreciate well-made furniture. It's just that we don't chill out on a sofa, watching TV or whatever else people commonly do there, so it just takes up room. And we want easy access to our cookbooks.

We gave up counting the number of cookbooks we own a long time ago. Gabriele and I collect them for slightly different reasons. I love books for the information they impart, but even more when they reflect a specific point in time or a person. I recently got a first edition of a seventies cookbook, *Les Diners de Gala*, written by Salvador Dalí and his wife, Gala, that is both inspiring and truly surreal, as one would expect from Dalí. At the opposite end of the sophistication scale, I have *Joys of Jell-O*, which always reminds me of my grandmother.

I learned about cooking and entertaining directly from my grandmother. I remember sitting on a stool next to her at the stove as she cooked and referred to her splattered and marked-up Betty Crocker cookbook. We loved watching Julia Child together. And she not only was a good cook, she knew how to set the stage for her dinner parties with a beautifully laid table and gorgeous centerpiece. And, since the chef is the star of the show, she always set aside a good piece of time to prepare herself in a lovely hostess gown and perfect makeup and hair. When Gabriele and I give a party, I put everything I learned from her into play.

Back to the *Joys of Jell-O*. My grandmother was a passionate maker of gelatin molds, and she knew every trick for the layering, tinting (with whipped cream or sour cream), and unmolding of towering, quivering desserts and salads. I understand from my daughter Giulia that Jell-O is making a comeback on tween cooking sites. I can't wait to break out the molds and make some Jell-O with her. I know—it's not very Italian!

My cookbook collection began when my mother gave me a handwritten book with all of my favorite family recipes. This book is truly a treasure and one of my prized possessions. I still tuck recipe clippings in it, and it "lives" in our kitchen drawer where I can see it whenever I want.

Growing up in New York, I was exposed to just about every kind of cuisine, and the best place to learn how to make something was from a cookbook. After tasting a dish at a friend's, I would research it in books. I appreciate a cookbook like a work of art—the weight of the paper, the lush photography, and the well-designed layout. Even though I can find recipes online, there is nothing like the satisfaction of holding a beautiful cookbook in your hands and browsing its pages for ideas and inspiration.

. . .

G: I like cookbooks that take me to another place. Although my cooking is Italian, sometimes I want to take a journey to a different cuisine. Right now, I have a stack of Turkish cookbooks that I am reading, and I'm thinking that a little saffron might be good in a pasta recipe I'm developing. I seem to gravitate toward Mediterranean-style cooking from warm climates. Olive oil is in my blood! I carefully choose a cookbook the same way I do a CD or record (yes, I still have some vinyl). I check it out, think it over, check it out again—and usually make some excuse to buy it anyway! Or, I'll obsess over a series and decide that I must have each one to complete the set. Anyone who has a cookbook collection will tell you that this is normal behavior.

In Italy, my primary cooking teachers were my grandmother, mother, and father, who taught me the basics. But there are two cookbooks in virtually every Tuscan household—Pellegrino Artusi's *La scienza in cucina e l'arte di mangiar bene* (*Science in the Kitchen and the Art of Eating Well*), more than 125 years old, and Ada Boni's *Il talismano della felicitá* (*The Talisman Italian Cookbook*), originally published in 1929—for reference for the times when you need an actual recipe. When people ask me why I cook like I do, with such attention to classic formulas, I think of how these two books, each with hundreds of recipes, have deeply influenced me. They taught me, and generations of other Italians, how to make a dish the "correct" way, and I am very careful about how I stray from their paths. To me, these recipes represent my heritage, if not me as a complete person, because I have been known to put a jalapeño in my mayonnaise, something that neither Artusi nor Boni would understand.

Don't ask me how we catalog our cookbooks—it's creative. We tend to put subjects together in separate areas of the bookcases or floor. We do have an antique metal bread cabinet to hold our baking books, including my favorite, Elisabeth M. Prueitt and Chad Robertson's *Tartine*, the book that taught me how to make the bread I bake every day for my family. That I learned how to make this loaf, which is now our family tradition, from a cookbook is the perfect illustration of why books are so important in our home.

PASTA AND RISOTTO

SPAGHETTI WITH SARDINES AND BREAD CRUMBS

Spaghetti con sardine e pangrattato

• •

Wine/Beer Pairing: Soave Classico or lager beer
Makes 4 to 6 servings

G: *This recipe always reminds me of my grandfather Renato. He had a little seaside place in Quer-cianella, just south of Livorno. (There is a big Jewish community in the area, and there are a lot of fam-ilies named Corcos!) After a day at the beach, he didn't always feel like making a complicated dinner. Although he had a wide array of freshly caught seafood literally outside his door, he'd rummage through the pantry for a can of sardines and a box of pasta . . . and a tasty, filling meal was on the table in no time. When I'm hungry and don't know what to cook, this is the dish that comes to the rescue. It is a convincing reason to have a can of sardines in the pantry.*

4 tablespoons extra-virgin olive oil, plus more
    for serving
1 cup soft bread crumbs (process day-old bread
    in a blender or food processor)
1 tablespoon finely chopped fresh flat-leaf
    parsley, plus more for serving
One 3¾-ounce can boneless sardine fillets
    packed in olive oil, drained
2 tablespoons drained and coarsely chopped
    capers

3 garlic cloves, chopped
1 teaspoon finely chopped fresh thyme
Pinch of hot red pepper flakes
¼ cup dry white wine
1 pound spaghetti
Sea salt and freshly ground black pepper
Homemade Red Pepper Oil, for serving
    (optional, see Note, page 114)

1. Bring a large pot of salted water to a boil over high heat.

2. Meanwhile, heat 2 tablespoons of the olive oil in a large skillet over medium-high heat. Add the bread crumbs and cook, stirring often, until they are golden brown, about 2 minutes. Stir in the parsley. Turn the crumbs out onto a plate. Wipe out the skillet with paper towels.

3. Add the remaining 2 tablespoons olive oil with the sardines, capers, garlic, thyme, and red pepper flakes to the skillet and return to medium-high heat. Cook, stirring occasionally with a spoon and breaking up the sardines well, until the garlic is fragrant and softened, about 2 minutes. Stir in the wine and cook until it evaporates by half, about 1 minute. Remove the skillet from the heat.

4. Add the spaghetti to the water and cook, according to the package directions, until al dente. Scoop out and reserve about ½ cup of the pasta water. Drain the pasta well and transfer to a warm large serving bowl. Add the sardine sauce and toss, adding enough of the reserved cooking water to loosen the sauce. Season to taste with the salt and black pepper.

5. Divide the pasta equally among individual serving bowls. Top each with the bread-crumb mixture, a generous drizzle of olive oil, and additional parsley. Serve immediately with the red pepper oil, if using.

NOTE Homemade Red Pepper Oil is a deliciously spicy condiment for this pasta. To make it, slowly heat ½ cup extra-virgin olive oil with 4 dried red pepperoncini, crumbled, in a small saucepan over low heat until small bubbles form around the pepper flakes, 5 to 10 minutes. Remove from the heat and let cool. Strain through a fine-mesh wire sieve. If you wish, use a funnel to transfer the oil to a small bottle. The oil can be stored at room temperature for up to 2 days. For longer storage, up to 2 months, refrigerate the oil and bring to room temperature before serving.

SPAGHETTI WITH SHRIMP AND LEMON SAUCE

Spaghetti con gambieri e limone

●●●

Wine Pairing: Pinot Grigio
Makes 4 to 6 servings

D: *We have a very hectic household with two very active daughters and Mamma and Babbo busy with their careers. We know we are not alone. So, super-easy dinners are always welcome, and they don't get much easier than this one. Be careful not to overcook the shrimp when sautéing it, as it will cook even more when it is mixed with the hot pasta. This is one of the few dishes where Gabriele uses butter (to give a little body to the sauce), but you can substitute a flavorful finishing olive oil, if you prefer.*

1 pound spaghetti
4 tablespoons extra-virgin olive oil, plus more for serving
1 pound jumbo (21–25 count) shrimp, peeled and deveined
2 garlic cloves, thinly sliced
¼ teaspoon hot red pepper flakes

⅓ cup dry white wine
2 tablespoons fresh lemon juice
2 tablespoons finely chopped fresh flat-leaf parsley, plus more for serving
2 ounces (½ stick) unsalted butter, at room temperature
Sea salt and freshly ground black pepper

1. Bring a large pot of salted water to a boil over high heat. Add the spaghetti and cook, according to the package directions, until al dente.

2. Meanwhile, heat 2 tablespoons of the oil in a large skillet over medium-high heat. Add the shrimp and cook, tossing them occasionally, just until they turn opaque around the edges, 2 to 3 minutes. Do not overcook the shrimp as they will heat and cook more when tossed with the hot pasta. Transfer to a plate and tent with aluminum foil to keep warm.

3. With the skillet off the heat, add the remaining 2 tablespoons oil and the garlic with the red pepper flakes. (The skillet is already very hot, so it is important to add the garlic and oil together, off the heat, to keep the garlic from browning too fast.) Stir constantly until the garlic softens, about 1 minute. Return the skillet to medium heat. Add the wine and lemon juice and bring to a boil. Stir in the parsley and remove from the heat.

4. Drain the spaghetti and return to the cooking pot. Scrape in the garlic mixture, add the reserved shrimp and the butter and toss well. Season to taste with the salt and black pepper. Transfer to bowls, sprinkle with additional parsley, and serve hot with extra oil on the side for drizzling.

PAPPARDELLE WITH ASPARAGUS AND MUSHROOMS

Pappardelle con asparagi e funghi

• •

Makes 4 to 6 servings

G: *When spring arrives and you have great asparagus, this light, vegetarian pasta should go to the top of your "must cook" list. Take advantage of seasonal mushrooms too—while we make this most often with reliable cremini from the supermarket, it is terrific with more elusive chanterelles or morels. The ricotta is a nice touch if you want a bit more creaminess. I serve it on the side.*

3 tablespoons extra-virgin olive oil

1 large garlic clove, crushed

10 ounces full-flavored mushrooms, such as cremini, chanterelles, or morels, sliced

1½ pounds thin asparagus, woody ends discarded

2 teaspoons finely chopped fresh *nipitella* or 1 teaspoon finely chopped fresh mint, plus more for serving

Sea salt and freshly ground black pepper

1 pound pappardelle, fettuccine, or other wide, flat pasta

½ cup freshly grated Parmigiano-Reggiano cheese, plus more for serving

1 cup fresh ricotta cheese, at room temperature

High-quality extra-virgin olive oil, for finishing

1. Bring a large pot of salted water to a boil over high heat.

2. Position a rack in the center of the oven and preheat the oven to 425°F.

3. Heat 2 tablespoons of the oil with the garlic in a large skillet over medium-high heat. Cook, occasionally turning the garlic, until it turns golden brown, about 2 minutes. Discard the garlic. Add the mushrooms and cook, stirring occasionally, until the mushrooms are beginning to brown but still juicy, about 8 minutes. (Wild mushrooms will give off a good amount of liquid that needs to boil away before they can brown, so they will take longer.)

4. Meanwhile, toss the asparagus with the remaining 1 tablespoon oil on a large rimmed baking sheet. Bake, occasionally rolling the asparagus on the sheet to turn them, until the asparagus is just crisp-tender, about 10 minutes, depending on the thickness of the spears. Transfer to a chopping board and cut into 1- to 2-inch lengths. Add to the skillet with the mushrooms. Season with the *nipitella* and the salt and pepper to taste. Cover with the lid ajar to keep warm.

5. Add the pappardelle to the boiling water and cook, according to the package directions, until al dente. Scoop out and reserve about ½ cup of the cooking water. Drain the pasta well and return to its cooking pot. Add the mushroom mixture and the Parmigiano. Mix, adding enough of the hot cooking water to make a creamy sauce. Season again to taste with the salt and pepper. Divide among individual bowls and add a dollop of ricotta to the side of each mound of pasta. Sprinkle with *nipitella*, drizzle with the finishing olive oil, and serve, with additional Parmigiano on the side.

PASTA WITH GARBANZO BEANS

Pasta e ceci

• •

Wine Pairing: Greco di Tufo

Makes 4 to 6 servings

Pasta e ceci is one of the best examples of having a well-stocked pantry. We are realizing that this chapter has a lot of super-quick pasta dishes, and it points out to us how many times we have to get dinner on the table fast! This is yet another pasta that has saved us when we thought we didn't have food in the house for dinner. And it is also why you will always find some guanciale or pancetta (which both last for months) in our fridge! Some cooks make their pasta e ceci *with tomatoes, but we prefer this back-to-basics approach.*

1 medium red onion, cut into thin half-moons
½ cup (¼-inch) diced guanciale or pancetta
2 tablespoons extra-virgin olive oil
2 garlic cloves, finely chopped
Two 15-ounce cans garbanzo beans (chickpeas)
Sea salt and freshly ground black pepper

1 pound ditalini or other short tubular pasta
Finely chopped fresh flat-leaf parsley, for serving
Freshly grated Parmigiano-Reggiano cheese, for serving

1. Bring a large pot of salted water to a boil over high heat.

2. Cook the onion, guanciale, and oil in a large skillet over medium heat, stirring occasionally, until the onion is golden brown, about 5 minutes. Add the garlic and cook until it is fragrant, about 1 minute.

3. Drain the garbanzo beans in a sieve over a medium bowl, reserving the liquid. Puree 1 cup of the garbanzo beans and all of the liquid in a blender.

4. Add the garbanzo bean puree and the remaining garbanzo beans to the skillet. Bring to a simmer, crushing the beans with a wooden spoon. Simmer until the sauce thickens slightly, about 5 minutes. Season to taste with the salt and pepper. Keep the sauce warm over very low heat.

5. While the sauce is cooking, add the ditalini to water and cook, according to the package directions, until al dente. Scoop out and reserve about ½ cup of the cooking water. Drain the pasta well and return to its cooking pot. Add the garbanzo bean sauce and stir over low heat, adding enough of the reserved cooking liquid to give the sauce a creamy consistency. Spoon into bowls and sprinkle with parsley. Serve with the Parmigiano on the side.

RIGATONI WITH WINTER SQUASH, SAUSAGE, AND KALE

Rigatoni con zucca, salciccia, e cavolo nero

• •

Wine Pairing: Teroldego
Makes 4 to 6 servings

In Tuscany, cooks don't have a lot of uses for hard-shelled winter squash. It is typically roasted as a side dish or turned into soup. At our Brooklyn farmer's market in autumn and winter, the stands are filled with a huge variety of squashes, each one more attractive and tasty than the other. Here, we cook with squash all the time, and the entire family benefits. This pasta balances the somewhat sweet squash with sausage, kale, and Romano cheese. The smooth shape of butternut squash makes it easy to work with, but you can substitute your favorite (such as kabocha).

3 tablespoons extra-virgin olive oil, plus more
    for the baking sheet and serving
1 small butternut squash (about 2 pounds)
Sea salt and freshly ground black pepper
8 ounces sweet or spicy Italian sausage, about
    2 links, casings removed
Two 3-inch sprigs fresh rosemary
1 medium red onion, chopped

1 garlic clove, minced
½ cup dry white wine, such as Pinot Grigio
One 7-ounce bunch black (also called lacinato,
    Tuscan, or dinosaur) kale, tough stems
    discarded and leaves coarsely chopped
1 pound rigatoni
½ cup freshly grated Pecorino Romano cheese,
    plus more for serving

1. Position a rack in the center of the oven and preheat the oven to 400°F. Lightly oil a large rimmed baking sheet.

2. Peel and seed the squash. Cut the flesh into ½-inch cubes. Measure out 3 cups cubed squash and reserve the remainder for another use. (We always seem to have leftover squash. You might want to roast all of it and save the leftover squash to add to salads or stir into cooked rice.)

3. Toss the squash and 2 tablespoons of the oil on the prepared baking sheet. Season to taste with the salt and pepper. Bake, stirring occasionally, until the squash is tender and tinged with brown, 25 to 30 minutes. Keep warm in a turned-off oven with the oven door ajar.

4. Meanwhile, heat the remaining tablespoon of oil in a large skillet over medium-high heat. Add the sausage and rosemary and cook, stirring occasionally and breaking up the meat with the side of the spoon into bite-sized pieces, until the sausage is browned, if not cooked through, about 6 minutes. Move the sausage and rosemary to one side of the skillet. Add the onion and garlic to the opposite side of the skillet and reduce the heat to medium low. Cook, stirring just the onion mixture occasionally, until softened, about 3 minutes. Mix the ingredients together and continue cooking to blend the flavors, about 3 minutes. Increase the heat to high, stir in the wine, and

bring it to a boil. Discard the rosemary sprigs. Stir in the kale and return the heat to medium low. Cook until the kale is just tender, about 6 minutes. Remove from the heat. Add the squash and cover to keep warm.

5. While the sausage mixture is cooking, bring a large pot of salted water to a boil over high heat. Add the rigatoni and cook, according to the package directions, until al dente. Scoop out and reserve about ½ cup of the cooking water. Drain the pasta well and return to the cooking pot.

6. Add the sausage mixture and Romano cheese to the rigatoni and mix well, adding enough of the reserved cooking water to make a light sauce. Spoon into individual bowls, top with a drizzle of oil, and serve, with additional Romano passed on the side.

CHEESE AND PEPPER PASTA

Cacio e pepe

• •

Wine Pairing: Rosso dei Castelli Romani

Makes 4 to 6 servings

Just about every trattoria in Rome serves cacio e pepe *("cheese and pepper"). It may be a typical Roman dish, but every Italian, from the toe to the top of the "boot" knows how to make it. The traditional cheese used is Pecorino Romano. However, it is little too sharp and salty for our family's taste; we prefer to mellow it out with some Parmigiano. It took a long time for* cacio e pepe *to become known on these shores—maybe because it was* too *simple? But once Americans learned to love real, freshly grated Parmigiano and Romano (as opposed to the pre-ground, shelf-stable kind), a new pasta star was born on these shores too. Dinner doesn't get much easier—or delicious—than this super-simple pasta.*

1 pound long pasta, such as bucatini, spaghetti, or long fusilli

½ cup freshly grated Parmigiano-Reggiano cheese

½ cup freshly grated Romano cheese, plus more for serving

Freshly ground coarse black pepper

Extra-virgin olive oil, for serving

1. Bring a large pot of salted water to a boil over high heat. Add the pasta and cook, according to the package directions, until al dente. Scoop out and reserve about ½ cup of the cooking liquid. Drain the pasta and return it to the hot cooking pot.

2. Mix the Parmigiano and Romano cheeses together. Tossing the pasta, gradually add the cheese mixture to the pot so it melts easily without clumping, adding enough of the reserved cooking liquid to make a creamy sauce. Mix in a generous amount of the pepper. The cheeses are salty, so you probably won't need any salt.

3. Serve the pasta in individual bowls, topping each serving with a drizzle of oil. Pass around more of the Romano cheese at the table.

TIP It is important to gradually add the cheese in a few batches so it melts evenly. Do not dump it in all at once, or it will clump.

WAGON WHEELS WITH ZUCCHINI AND BRIE

Rotelle con zucchine e brie

• •

Wine Pairing: Pinot Bianco
Makes 4 to 6 servings

There is a lot to be said for long-simmered ragù, but let's also hear it for a pasta topping that can be made in the time it takes for the cooking water to come to a boil. This creamy cheesy zucchini mixture makes the most of something you may have on hand, supermarket Brie. Not everyone in our family likes the edible rind, so we usually trim it off, but you can leave it on for more texture. Cook the zucchini and onion over moderate heat, because if they brown too deeply, they will be more sweet than savory.

2 tablespoons extra-virgin olive oil
5 medium zucchini, about 1½ pounds, cut
    into ⅛ inch rounds (a mandoline or plastic
    V-slicer do a good job for this)
1 medium red onion, thinly sliced
12 ounces Brie, cut into 1-inch chunks, rind
    trimmed as desired

1 pound wheel-shaped pasta, or tube-shaped
    pasta such as penne or ziti
Sea salt and freshly ground black pepper
Freshly grated Parmigiano-Reggiano cheese, for
    serving

1. Bring a large pot of salted water to a boil over high heat.

2. Meanwhile, heat the oil in a very large skillet over medium heat. Spread the zucchini in the skillet and sprinkle the onion on top. Cook, stirring about every 5 minutes, until the zucchini is tender and barely beginning to brown, 15 to 20 minutes. Remove from the heat. Scatter the Brie over the vegetables and cover while cooking the pasta to warm and soften the cheese.

3. Add the pasta to the boiling water and cook, according to the package directions, until al dente. Scoop out and reserve ½ cup of the cooking water. Drain the pasta well.

4. Return the pasta to its cooking pot. Add the zucchini mixture. Toss, adding as much of the reserved cooking water as needed to make a light and creamy sauce. Season to taste with the salt and pepper. Serve hot with the Parmigiano on the side.

BAKED TRUFFLE CAVATAPPI

Pasta al forno con formaggio tartufato

• •

Wine Pairing: Full-bodied super Tuscan from Bolgheri
Makes 6 to 8 servings

For a family-style macaroni and cheese, we make pasta ai quattro formaggi *from our first book. But for a special, grown-up occasion, this truffled version is the one we serve. The defining ingredient is truffle-flavored cheese, of which there are several options. For the deepest flavor, look for one that has visible bits of truffle, such as* boschetto al tartufo, *a creamy cheese made from both sheep's and cow's milk that melts like a dream. This recipe uses* besciamella *(béchamel or white sauce) as the base, with the cheese melted in. Serve the pasta in relatively small portions (it's especially good baked in individual containers), because it is very rich, and probably best as a separate* primi *course at a traditional Italian dinner.*

PASTA
Softened unsalted butter, for the dish
1 pound cavatappi or other tube-shaped pasta
2 tablespoons unsalted butter
2 tablespoons unbleached all-purpose flour
3 cups whole milk, heated until steaming
8 ounces *boschetto al tartufo* cheese, cut into
  small cubes
Sea salt and freshly ground black pepper
⅛ teaspoon freshly grated nutmeg

BREAD CRUMBS
¼ cup plain dried bread crumbs
¼ cup freshly grated Parmigiano-Reggiano
  cheese
1 tablespoon unsalted butter, melted

1. Position a rack in the center of the oven and preheat the oven to 350°F. Lightly butter a 9 by 13-inch baking dish.

2. Bring a large pot of salted water to a boil over high heat. Add the cavatappi and cook, stirring occasionally, until the pasta is just short of al dente, about 2 minutes less than the recommended cooking time on the package directions. The pasta will be cooked again in the oven, so it is important not to overcook it. Drain well and return to the cooking pot.

3. Meanwhile, melt the butter in a medium saucepan over medium heat. Whisk in the flour. Reduce the heat to low and let bubble without browning for 1 minute. Gradually whisk in the hot milk and bring to a simmer. Cook, whisking often, until the sauce is lightly thickened and no raw flour taste remains, about 5 minutes. Remove from the heat. Add the cheese and let it soften in the sauce for about 3 minutes. Whisk until the cheese melts and the sauce is smooth. Season the sauce to taste with the salt and pepper and stir in the nutmeg. Mix the pasta and sauce together in the pasta cooking pot. Spread in the prepared baking dish.

4. To prepare the bread crumbs: Mix the bread crumbs and Parmigiano well in a small bowl. Add the melted butter and mix with your fingertips until combined. Sprinkle evenly over the pasta.

5. Bake until the pasta is lightly browned, 20 to 30 minutes. Let stand for 5 minutes, then serve hot.

TIP *Boschetto al tartufo* is our preferred cheese for this dish because it is rindless (meaning no waste) and has plenty of real truffles. It is sold at well-stocked cheese stores. Supermarkets sometimes carry other kinds of truffled cheeses, but these often are made with artificially flavored truffle oil. Most truffle oil has never been near a real truffle, and we don't use it.

AUTUMN LASAGNA WITH RADICCHIO, MUSHROOMS, AND GORGONZOLA

Lasagne d'autunno

• • • • • • • • • • • • • • • • • • • •

Wine Pairing: Marzemino or Nero d'Avola

Makes 9 servings

G: *For a wintertime vegetarian pasta that will warm you right through, make this "white" lasagna without any tomato sauce. (Though the white sauce, besciamella, is better known by its French name, béchamel, some historians believe it was probably created by Italian chefs.) We admit that this pasta, like most lasagna, is a labor of love, but so worth the effort. If you have serious blue cheese haters to serve, substitute Gruyère or fontina for the Gorgonzola. The sage butter is a nice touch, but you could simply sprinkle each serving with some freshly chopped sage. (I think that cooking the herb in some butter helps smooth out its rough, piney flavor.)*

BESCIAMELLA

3 ounces (¾ stick) unsalted butter
⅓ cup plus 1 tablespoon (55 grams)
    unbleached all-purpose flour
4 cups whole milk, heated
⅛ teaspoon freshly grated nutmeg
1½ cups (6 ounces) crumbled Gorgonzola dulce
Sea salt and freshly ground black pepper

Softened unsalted butter, for the baking dish
9 no-boil lasagna noodles (about half of one
    9-ounce box)
1½ cups (6 ounces) freshly grated Parmigiano-
    Reggiano cheese
4 tablespoons plain dried bread crumbs

FILLING

3 tablespoons unsalted butter
1 pound cremini mushrooms, thinly sliced
1 large yellow onion, chopped
3 garlic cloves, minced
2 large heads radicchio, cored and thinly sliced
    (about 1½ pounds)
Sea salt and freshly ground black pepper

SAGE BUTTER

3 ounces (¾ stick) unsalted butter
16 sage leaves, cut into thin shreds

1. To make the *besciamella:* Melt the butter in a medium saucepan over medium-low heat. Whisk in the flour and let it bubble without browning for 1 minute. Whisk in the warm milk and nutmeg and bring to a simmer. Reduce the heat to low and simmer, whisking often to avoid scorching, until smooth and thickened, about 10 minutes. Remove from the heat. Add the Gorgonzola, let stand for about 1 minute, and whisk to melt the cheese. Season to taste with the salt and pepper. Set the sauce aside.

2. Meanwhile, to make the filling: Melt the butter in a large skillet over medium-high heat. Add the mushrooms and cook, stirring occasionally, until they give off their juices and begin to brown, about 6 minutes. Move the mushrooms to one side of the skillet. Add the onion and garlic to the empty side and cook, occasionally stirring the onion mixture (but not the mushrooms) until they are beginning to soften, about 2 to 3 minutes. Stir the vegetables together. A handful at a time, stir in the radicchio and cook until it wilts before adding more. Cook until the radicchio is tender, about 5 minutes. Season to taste with the salt and pepper. Remove from the heat.

3. Position a rack in the center of the oven and preheat the oven to 350°F. Lightly butter a 9 by 13-inch flameproof baking dish. (We have an enameled cast-iron lasagna pan that we love.) Spread about ⅓ cup of the *besciamella* on the bottom of the dish. Add 3 noodles to cover the sauce, taking care that the noodles do not overlap. (They will expand during cooking.) Cover with about one-third of the remaining sauce, one-half of the radicchio mixture, and ½ cup of the Parmigiano cheese. Sprinkle with 2 tablespoons of the bread crumbs. Repeat with 3 more noodles, another third of the sauce, and the remaining radicchio filling, ½ cup Parmigiano, and the remaining 2 tablespoons bread crumbs. Finish with the remaining noodles, spread with the remaining sauce, and sprinkle with the remaining ½ cup Parmigiano. Cover the dish tightly with aluminum foil.

4. Bake for 30 minutes. Uncover and continue baking until the sauce is bubbling, about 20 minutes more. Remove the lasagna from the oven.

5. Position a broiler rack about 8 inches from the source of heat and preheat the broiler on high. Broil the lasagna until the top is lightly browned, watching carefully to avoid burning, about 2 minutes. Remove from the broiler and let stand for 10 minutes.

6. Meanwhile, to make the sage butter: Heat the butter in a small skillet over medium heat until the foam subsides. Add the sage and cook, stirring often, until the sage crisps, about 1 minute. Remove from the heat.

7. Cut the lasagna into portions and transfer to individual serving bowls. Drizzle each serving with some of the sage butter and serve.

LAYERED POLENTA WITH BROCCOLI RABE

Polenta pasticciata vegetariana

●●●

Wine Pairing: Young Sangiovese
Makes 6 to 8 main course or 10 to 12 appetizer servings

Soft-cooked polenta is often served as a side dish to sauced main courses. But when it is cooled and allowed to firm up, it can be sliced into slabs that can be layered with tomato sauce and mozzarella, just like lasagna. Some people like to serve this as a vegetarian main course, but we also serve it cut into small portions as an appetizer. Either way, "polenta as lasagna" is virtually unknown in America, and always sparks a conversation about how delicious it is! The broccoli rabe filling is wonderful, but consider other vegetables like grilled eggplant, sautéed mushrooms, or steamed and squeezed-dry spinach.

POLENTA
Extra-virgin olive oil, for oiling the pan
1 teaspoon sea salt
2 cups instant polenta

BROCCOLI RABE
2 pounds broccoli rabe
2 tablespoons extra-virgin olive oil
2 garlic cloves, coarsely chopped

SAUCE
3 tablespoons extra-virgin olive oil, plus more
    for the baking dish
1 small red onion, chopped
2 garlic cloves, minced
¼ teaspoon hot red pepper flakes
One 28-ounce can peeled tomatoes in juice,
    pureed with their juice in a blender
¼ cup coarsely chopped fresh basil
Sea salt and freshly ground black pepper

1 pound fresh mozzarella cheese, shredded
    (see Tip, page 169)
1 cup freshly grated Parmigiano-Reggiano
    cheese

1. To cook the polenta: Lightly oil a 9 by 5-inch loaf pan. Bring 6 cups of water and the salt to a boil in a medium heavy-bottomed saucepan over high heat. Slowly whisk in the polenta, making sure the mixture is smooth. Change over to a wooden spoon and stir constantly until the polenta comes to a boil. Cook according to the package directions, stirring often, until smooth and thickened. Spread the polenta in the loaf pan (it will be very full). Let cool until tepid, about 1 hour. Invert and unmold onto a cutting board, and let cool completely, about 2 hours more.

2. To cook the broccoli rabe: Bring a large saucepan of salted water to a boil over high heat. Add the broccoli rabe and return to a boil. Cook until crisp-tender, about 5 minutes. Drain well.

3. Heat the oil with the garlic in a large skillet over medium heat until the garlic is fragrant and softened, about 2 minutes. A handful at a time, stir in the broccoli rabe. Cover the skillet and reduce the heat to medium low. Cook, stirring occasionally, until the broccoli rabe is tender, about

15 minutes. Transfer to a colander and let it drain and cool. Coarsely chop the broccoli rabe and drain again to remove any excess liquid.

4. Meanwhile, to make the sauce: Cook the onion and oil in a large saucepan over medium heat, stirring often, until the onion is tender but not browned, about 4 minutes. Stir in the garlic and cook until it is fragrant, about 1 minute. Stir in the red pepper flakes, followed by the pureed tomatoes, and bring to a simmer over high heat. Reduce the heat to medium low and simmer, stirring occasionally, until the sauce has slightly reduced, about 20 minutes. During the last few minutes, stir in the basil. Season to taste with the salt and pepper.

5. Position a rack in the center of the oven and preheat the oven to 350°F. Lightly oil a flameproof 9 by 13-inch baking dish.

6. Cut the polenta crosswise into 30 slices about ¼ inch thick. Arrange 10 of the polenta slices in a single layer in the dish, trimming them as needed to fit the dish and fill in gaps. Top with one-half of the broccoli rabe, followed by one-third each of the sauce, mozzarella, and Parmigiano. Repeat with another layer of polenta, the rest of the broccoli rabe, sauce, mozzarella, and Parmigiano. Finish with the remaining ingredients. (The dish can be covered loosely with plastic wrap and kept at room temperature for up to 2 hours. Remove the plastic wrap before baking.)

7. Place the baking dish on a baking sheet. Bake, uncovered, until the mozzarella is melted and the juices are bubbling, about 50 minutes. Remove from the oven.

8. Position a broiler rack about 8 inches from the source of heat and preheat the broiler on high. Return the dish to the oven and broil just until the mozzarella topping is golden brown, 1 to 2 minutes. Let stand for 10 minutes. Cut into serving portions and serve hot.

POTATO GNOCCHI WITH BUTTERY RED SAUCE

Gnocchi di patate al burro e pomodoro

••

Wine Pairing: Vernaccia

Makes 6 servings

Nothing beats homemade potato gnocchi. They are a pleasure to make, but try to enlist an extra pair (or more) of hands to make the rolling go quicker. This is a fun family project. The last time we made them, Giulia couldn't resist trying her hand at shaping the little pillows. We realized then that part of the fun of homemade gnocchi is that they are all different sizes, unlike those in the perfectly molded packages at the supermarket! If your hand-formed gnocchi are irregular, don't worry. You will often find potato gnocchi simply tossed with sage sautéed in butter, but we love this red sauce, which uses butter to lend it richness. Gabriele's Nonna Lola always says potato dishes are better with butter, but that's because Nonna Lola is from Venice, and Venetians love their butter! In this dish, we agree.

BUTTERY RED SAUCE
1 tablespoon extra-virgin olive oil
½ medium red onion, cut into thin half-moons
3 tablespoons unsalted butter
One 28-ounce can peeled tomatoes in juice, pureed with their juice in a blender
¼ cup coarsely chopped fresh basil
Sea salt and freshly ground black pepper

POTATO GNOCCHI
1 pound baking potatoes, such as russets, scrubbed but unpeeled
3 large egg yolks
¼ teaspoon sea salt
1½ cups (210 grams) unbleached all-purpose flour, plus more for dusting and shaping dough

Fresh basil leaves, for serving
Freshly grated Parmigiano-Reggiano cheese, for serving

1. To make the sauce: Heat the oil in a medium saucepan over medium heat. Add the onion and cook, stirring occasionally, until it is tender but not browned, about 6 minutes. Add the butter and stir until it is melted. Stir in the pureed tomatoes and bring to a simmer. Reduce the heat to medium low and cook, stirring occasionally, until slightly reduced and thickened, about 25 minutes. During the last few minutes, stir in the basil. Season to taste with the salt and pepper. Remove from the heat. The sauce can be cooled, covered, and refrigerated for up to 2 days. Reheat over low heat before using.

2. To make the gnocchi: Put the potatoes in a large saucepan and add enough salted water to cover by 1 inch. Cover the saucepan and bring to a boil over high heat. Reduce the heat to low and simmer, with the lid ajar, until the potatoes are tender when pierced with the tip of a small knife, about 25 minutes, depending on the size of the potatoes. Drain the potatoes, cool until easy to handle, and remove the peels.

3. Put the potatoes through a ricer into a medium bowl. (Or rub the potatoes with a wooden spoon through a coarse-mesh wire sieve into the bowl.) Let cool until tepid, about 20 minutes. Don't rush this step, as you want the potatoes to give off as much steam and moisture as possible. Beat the egg yolks and salt into the potatoes. Using a wooden spoon, gradually stir in the flour until the mixture forms a smooth, stiff dough. The dough will be tacky. Don't add more flour, as it absorbs more during shaping. Cover and refrigerate the dough until lightly chilled, about 1 hour.

4. Generously flour a work surface and dust a rimmed baking sheet with flour. Working with a piece of dough about the size of a large lemon, place the dough on the work surface. Grab the dough and squeeze it into a rough log. Place the dough back on the work surface. With your hands placed lightly on top of the dough, roll the dough back and forth, moving your hands apart as your roll, to shape it into a smooth rope about ¾ inch wide. Cut the dough into ¾-inch pieces and transfer to the baking sheet. Repeat until all of the dough has been cut. The gnocchi can be covered with plastic wrap and refrigerated for up to 8 hours. To freeze them, first put the gnocchi in the freezer until they are hard, about 4 hours. Transfer the individual frozen gnocchi to zip-tight plastic bags and freeze for up to 2 months. (Do not thaw the frozen gnocchi before cooking.)

5. Bring a large pot of salted water to a boil over high heat. Gradually add the gnocchi, stirring gently to keep them from sticking to each other. Cook until the gnocchi all rise to the surface of the water and continue cooking until the gnocchi are cooked through, 2 to 3 minutes more. Using a wire spider or sieve, transfer the gnocchi to a large serving bowl. (Using the spider to drain the gnocchi is much gentler than draining the delicate gnocchi in a colander. If you must use a colander, drain the contents of the pot very carefully to keep the gnocchi from breaking.)

6. Add about half of the tomato sauce to the gnocchi and fold them together with a rubber spatula, taking care not to break the gnocchi. Serve in individual bowls and sprinkle each with the basil. Serve immediately, with the Parmigiano and leftover tomato sauce on the side. The remaining sauce can be refrigerated for up to 3 days or frozen for up to 2 months.

TIP A potato ricer is an inexpensive and very useful tool. You may think that you don't need one, but it will make chores like preparing potatoes for these gnocchi (as well as the Potato Croquettes and Mashed Potatoes with Mascarpone on pages 217 and 222) very quick and easy.

SAUSAGE AND CHIANTI RISOTTO

Risotto con salciccia e Chianti

● ●

Makes 4 servings

Ever heard the advice to never cook with a wine you wouldn't drink? With this hearty risotto you have a chance to put that dictum into action, because if you open a bottle to cook with it, you will have left-overs. We always put Parmigiano rind into the pot to release flavor and nuttiness into the risotto.

6 cups Large Batch Vegetable Broth (page 67)
1 tablespoon extra-virgin olive oil
1 tablespoon unsalted butter
8 ounces sweet Italian sausage, casings removed, crumbled into small pieces
One 6-inch sprig fresh rosemary
2 garlic cloves, unpeeled

1½ cups rice for risotto, such as arborio or vialone nano
1 cup hearty red wine, preferably Chianti
One 3-inch-square piece Parmigiano-Reggiano rind (optional)
½ cup freshly grated Parmigiano-Reggiano cheese, plus more for serving
Sea salt and freshly ground black pepper

1. Bring the stock to a simmer in a medium saucepan over medium heat. Reduce the heat to its lowest setting to keep the broth warm while making the risotto.

2. Heat the oil and butter together in a large nonstick skillet over medium heat. Add the sausage, rosemary, and garlic and cook, occasionally stirring and breaking up the meat with the side of the spoon to be sure it is very well crumbled, until the sausage is lightly browned and the rosemary leaves are crisped, 7 to 10 minutes. Using a slotted spoon, transfer the sausage and rosemary to a plate, leaving any fat and the garlic cloves in the skillet.

3. Add the rice and cook, stirring often, until it begins to turn opaque, about 1 minute. Stir in the wine and bring to a simmer. From this point on, you must stir the risotto constantly, not only to keep it from scorching in the skillet but also to coax the starch out of the rice and give the sauce its creaminess. Reduce the heat until the risotto is cooking at a steady but not fast simmer. Stir until the wine is reduced by half, about 2 minutes. Add about ¾ cup of the hot broth into the risotto and stir until it is reduced by about two-thirds, about 2 minutes. Add the Parmigiano rind, if using. Repeat the procedure, adding the hot broth in ¾-cup increments, stirring constantly until the liquid reduces by two-thirds, and the rice is al dente, 18 to 20 minutes. During the last few minutes, add the sausage (but not the rosemary) to the risotto. Just before removing the skillet from the heat, stir the grated Parmigiano into the risotto. Season to taste with the salt and pepper. Discard the garlic and Parmigiano rind.

4. Remove the rosemary leaves from the reserved sprig. Spoon the risotto into individual bowls. Coarsely crumble the rosemary leaves over the risotto and serve, with more Parmigiano on the side.

RISOTTO TUTORIAL

In our household, creamy and filling risotto is every bit as popular as pasta. We offer two risotto recipes in this book that may share some common ingredients, but are actually quite different. The Sausage and Chianti Risotto on page 137 is a meaty, hearty example of the genre, and perfect for a winter meal. But the Zucchini and Radicchio Risotto (page 141, and pictured below) is vegetarian and quite light.

1. Stir the Italian rice (a starchy variety, such as arborio, vialone nano, or carnaroli) into a buttery base.

2. Once the rice is hot, add the wine—the burst of heat will cook away much of the raw alcohol flavor.

3. Gradually ladle warm broth into the risotto to maintain a steady simmer, stirring constantly for even cooking.

4. Add a chunk of Parmigiano rind to slowly melt and lend its rich, unique flavor into the simmering risotto.

5. Be sure to remove the rind before serving. You can rinse, refrigerate, and reuse the rind if you are feeling thrifty.

6. Just before serving, stir previously cooked ingredients (here, zucchini and radicchio) into the risotto.

ZUCCHINI AND RADICCHIO RISOTTO

Risotto di zucchine e radicchio

• •

Wine Pairing: Pinot Grigio
Makes 4 to 6 servings

G: *This vegetarian risotto is very satisfying. It's a wonderful balance of the sweet zucchini and onion with the slightly bitter radicchio, brought together with the slightly sharp Parmigiano. Be sure to let the zucchini cook until it is nicely browned, otherwise you won't get the lightly caramelized flavor that makes this so special. It takes time and patience to coax the browning into play, so don't rush this step.*

D: *Just as apples mean fall fruit, radicchio is a sign of autumn. I love it in pasta, risotto, roasted . . . and I love it in salads too!*

3 tablespoons extra-virgin olive oil
1 pound zucchini, cut into ¾-inch dice
2 tablespoons unsalted butter
1 medium yellow onion, cut into thin half-moons
6 cups Large Batch Vegetable Broth (page 67), plus more as needed
1½ cups rice for risotto, such as arborio or vialone nano
1 cup dry white wine, such as Pinot Grigio
One 3-inch-square piece Parmigiano-Reggiano rind (optional)
½ head radicchio, cored and cut crosswise into thin shreds (about 1½ cups)
1 cup freshly grated Parmigiano-Reggiano cheese, plus more for serving
Sea salt and freshly ground black pepper
High-quality extra-virgin olive oil, for finishing

1. Heat 2 tablespoons of the oil in a large, wide skillet over medium heat. Add the zucchini, spreading the pieces in a single layer as well as you can. Cook, without stirring, until the undersides are lightly browned, about 5 minutes. Be patient—you want the zucchini to brown. Toss the zucchini (if you must stir them, do so very gently so they don't break up) and continue cooking, tossing occasionally, until they are lightly browned all over, 8 to 10 minutes more. Transfer the zucchini to a plate and set aside.

2. Melt the butter with the remaining tablespoon oil in the skillet with the onion. Cook, stirring occasionally, until the onion is tender and beginning to brown, 4 or 5 minutes.

3. Meanwhile bring the broth to a simmer in a medium saucepan over medium heat. Reduce the heat to its lowest setting to keep the broth warm while making the risotto.

4. Add the rice to the skillet and cook, stirring often, until it begins to turn opaque, about 1 minute. Stir in the wine and bring to a simmer. From this point on, you must stir the risotto constantly. Add the Parmigiano rind, if using. Reduce the heat until the liquid is boiling at a steady but not

fast pace. Stir until the wine is reduced by half, about 1 minute. Add about ¾ cup of the hot broth into the risotto and stir until it is reduced by half, about 2 minutes. Repeat the procedure, adding the hot broth in ¾-cup increments, stirring constantly until the liquid reduces by two-thirds and the rice is barely tender, 18 to 20 minutes. During the last minute, add the zucchini and radicchio. Using a silicone spatula, gently fold them into the risotto, taking care not to mash the zucchini. Just before removing the skillet from the heat, fold the grated Parmigiano into the risotto. Season to taste with the salt and pepper. Discard the Parmigiano rind.

5. Spoon into bowls. Sprinkle with a little grated Parmigiano, finish with a drizzle of the high-quality oil, and serve the risotto immediately.

SEAFOOD

SEA BASS WITH SICILIAN CHERRY TOMATO SAUCE

Spigola alla siciliana

• •

Wine Pairing: Trebbiano or Vermentino
Makes 4 servings

We've always lived in places where seafood is plentiful and loved by the local cooks. Tuscany isn't Sicily, we grant you, but it does have a coastline that keeps the citizens in good supply of fish. The sauce, which can be made in minutes, is a riff on the Southern Italian stalwart, puttanesca, but made with fresh cherry tomatoes. While this recipe calls for wild sea bass fillets, the pungent sauce would work with just about any fish, especially rich and oily varieties, such as mackerel or bluefish.

SICILIAN CHERRY TOMATO SAUCE
2 tablespoons extra-virgin olive oil
2 anchovy fillets in olive oil, drained and
    minced
2 garlic cloves, thinly sliced
½ cup pitted and coarsely chopped oil-cured
    black olives
2 tablespoons drained and chopped capers
⅛ teaspoon hot red pepper flakes
1 pound cherry tomatoes, halved
Sea salt and freshly ground black pepper

Extra-virgin olive oil, for oiling pan and
    brushing fillets
4 wild sea bass fillets (about 6 ounces each)
Sea salt and freshly ground black pepper
Finely chopped fresh flat-leaf parsley, for
    serving

1. To make the sauce: Heat the oil and anchovies in a large saucepan over medium heat, stirring often, until the anchovies are sizzling and broken down into a paste, about 2 minutes. Add the garlic and cook until it begins to brown around the edges, about 1 minute. Stir in the olives, capers, and red pepper flakes and cook until heated through, about 2 minutes. Stir in the cherry tomatoes and season to taste with the salt and pepper. Cook, stirring occasionally, until the tomatoes begin to break down, about 10 minutes. Set the sauce aside.

2. Oil a large ridged grilling pan and heat it over medium-high heat. Brush the sea bass on both sides with the oil and season with the salt and pepper. Place on the grill, skin side down, and grill until the underside is seared with grill marks, about 3 minutes. Flip the fish over and cook until the other side is seared and the flesh is opaque when pierced in the center with the tip of a small sharp knife, about 3 minutes more. Transfer each fillet to a dinner plate and top with a spoonful of the sauce. Sprinkle with the parsley and serve.

BAKED SNAPPER WITH SPINACH FILLING

Fagottini di dentice e spinaci

• •

Wine Pairing: Bianco di Pitigliano
Makes 4 servings

D: *This recipe shows off the simplicity of the best Italian cooking. With just a few ingredients, this dish of snapper fillets folded over freshly cooked spinach with raisins and pine nuts is ready to bake in no time at all. This is one of our favorite dinner entrées for the whole family, easy enough for a weeknight, but special enough for company. And last, but far from least . . . it is light without being boring.*

SPINACH FILLING

2 tablespoons pine nuts
2 tablespoons extra-virgin olive oil
1 garlic clove, minced
1 pound baby spinach, rinsed but not dried
Sea salt and freshly ground black pepper
2 tablespoons golden or dark seedless raisins

Extra-virgin olive oil, for oiling the dish and
   drizzling on the fillets
4 skinless snapper fillets (about 6 ounces each)
Sea salt and freshly ground black pepper
½ cup dry white wine, such as Pinot Grigio
1 tablespoon tomato paste
Lemon wedges, for serving

1. To make the filling: Heat a medium skillet over medium heat until hot. Add the pine nuts and cook, stirring occasionally, until toasted, about 2 minutes. Transfer to a plate.

2. Add the oil and garlic to the skillet and stir over medium heat until the garlic is softened, about 1 minute. A handful at a time, stir in the spinach, letting the first addition wilt before adding more. Reduce the heat to medium low and cook, stirring occasionally, until the spinach is tender, about 5 minutes. Season to taste with the salt and pepper. Transfer the spinach mixture to a large wire sieve and let it stand until cool enough to handle, about 10 minutes. Press the spinach with a wooden spoon to extract the excess liquid. Transfer to a chopping board and coarsely chop the spinach. Transfer to a medium bowl and stir in the pine nuts and raisins.

3. Position a rack in the center of the oven and preheat the oven to 400°F. Lightly oil a large baking dish to hold the fillets.

4. Put the fillets on a work surface, skinned side down. Season them lightly with the salt and pepper. Place one-fourth of the spinach mixture on each fillet, and fold in half crosswise to cover the spinach. Transfer the fillets to the prepared dish. Mix the wine and tomato paste in a small bowl to dissolve the paste. Pour it around the fish and drizzle the fillets with the oil.

5. Roast just until each fillet is opaque when flaked with the tip of a small sharp knife, 15 to 20 minutes. Serve hot, with the lemon wedges.

SWORDFISH WITH ORANGE SALAD

Pesce spada con insalata di arancia

••••••••••••••••••••••••••••••••••••••

Beer Pairing: Lager beer
Makes 4 servings

This is one of the easiest seafood entrées you'll ever make, yet one of the most satisfying and attractive. Swordfish has a meatiness that is nicely balanced by the other components of this salad: spicy arugula, cool mint, sweet oranges, and crunchy pine nuts. To give the dish an authentic Italian touch and a more dramatic look, use dark-fleshed, slightly tart blood oranges instead of the standard navels (although the latter work too).

2 tablespoons fresh lemon juice
¼ teaspoon sea salt, plus more for seasoning
Freshly ground black pepper
½ cup plus 1 tablespoon extra-virgin olive oil
3 oranges, preferably blood oranges, peeled and cut between the membranes to separate the segments (see step 1, page 71)

2 tablespoons pine nuts (see step 1, page 149), toasted and cooled
1 tablespoon finely sliced fresh mint
4 swordfish steaks, cut ¾ inch thick (about 6 ounces each)
5 ounces baby arugula

1. Whisk the lemon juice, ¼ teaspoon salt, and a few grindings of pepper in a small bowl. Gradually whisk in ½ cup of the oil to make a vinaigrette. Mix the orange segments, pine nuts, and mint with 1 tablespoon of the vinaigrette in another small bowl. Set the orange salsa and remaining vinaigrette aside.

2. Season the swordfish to taste with salt and pepper. Heat the remaining tablespoon oil in a very large skillet over medium-high heat. Add the swordfish and cook, turning once, until lightly browned and the flesh is opaque but still juicy when pierced at the skin with the tip of a sharp knife, 6 to 8 minutes. Transfer to a platter.

3. Toss the arugula with the remaining vinaigrette in a large bowl. Season to taste with the salt and pepper. Divide the salad among 4 dinner plates. Top each with a swordfish steak and one-quarter of the orange salsa. Serve immediately.

SPICY SHRIMP SAUTÉ WITH LIME

Gamberi saltati al lime

• •

Beer Pairing: India pale ale

Makes 4 servings

This quick shrimp sauté has a definite Californian vibe thanks to our time spent in Los Angeles. With lime, jalapeño, and cilantro, it inadvertently took a turn toward Mexican cuisine and would be good served with white rice and black beans on the side. These days, it is difficult to tell how large or how hot the jalapeño will be, so we start with a half, and add more toward the end, if we feel it needs more heat.

1 lime
1 tablespoon unsalted butter
1 tablespoon extra-virgin olive oil
3 garlic cloves, each cut in half lengthwise
1½ pounds jumbo (21–25 count) shrimp, peeled and deveined

½ jalapeño, seeded and minced
¼ cup dry white wine
Sea salt and freshly ground pepper
2 tablespoons finely chopped fresh cilantro or flat-leaf parsley

1. Finely grate the zest from the lime onto a small plate or a piece of waxed paper. Juice the lime; you need 2 tablespoons. Set the zest and juice aside.

2. Heat the butter and oil in a very large nonstick skillet over medium-high heat. When the foam subsides, add the garlic and cook until it is fragrant and beginning to brown, 1 to 2 minutes. Using a slotted spoon, remove and discard the garlic.

3. Increase the heat to high. Add the shrimp and jalapeño to the skillet. Cook, stirring occasionally, just until the shrimp turn pink, about 3 minutes. Add the wine and let it cook until it is almost completely reduced, about 30 seconds. Stir in the reserved lime juice. Season to taste with the salt and pepper. Remove from the heat. Stir in the cilantro and the reserved lime zest and serve.

DEEP-FRIED SHRIMP WITH PINK SAUCE

Gamberoni fritti con salsa rosa

● ●

Makes 4 servings

G: Fritto misto *(a mix of battered and deep-fried seafood with vegetables)* is irresistible, but if I had to choose just one of its components, it would be the shrimp. The batter is simply flour and bread crumbs mixed with beer, and I don't think a better all-purpose coating for frying exists. I hardly ever measure the ingredients, as the recipe is embedded in my brain. The shrimp are especially tasty dipped in salsa rosa, *an Italian mayonnaise-based cocktail sauce tinted pink with tomato paste. The important thing to remember about deep-frying is not to skimp on the oil—the food should really "swim" in the pot. And remember to reheat the oil between batches.*

SALSA ROSA
1 tablespoon tomato paste
1 tablespoon lemon juice
½ cup Mayonnaise (page 158), homemade or
    store-bought
1 tablespoon finely chopped fresh chives
1 tablespoon prepared horseradish
Sea salt and freshly ground black pepper

DEEP-FRIED SHRIMP
Vegetable oil, for deep-frying
1¼ cups (175 grams) unbleached all-purpose
    flour
¼ cup plain dried bread crumbs
1¼ cups lager beer, such as Peroni, plus more
    as needed
1½ pounds jumbo (21–25 count) shrimp,
    peeled and deveined, tail segments intact

Lemon wedges, for serving

1. To make the *salsa rosa*: Whisk the tomato paste and lemon juice together in a small bowl to loosen the paste. Add the mayonnaise, chives, and horseradish and mix well. Season to taste with the salt and pepper. Cover and refrigerate to let the flavors blend, at least 1 hour and up to 1 day.

2. To make the deep-fried shrimp: Position a rack in the center of the oven and preheat the oven to 200°F. Line a large rimmed baking sheet with brown paper. Pour enough oil into a large, deep saucepan to come 2 inches up the sides. Heat over high heat until the oil reaches 350°F on a deep-frying thermometer.

3. Mix the flour and bread crumbs together in a large bowl. Stir in enough beer to make a batter that is a little thicker than heavy cream—it should cling well to the shrimp and not run off when dipped. In batches without crowding, dip the shrimp in the batter, letting the excess batter drip back into the bowl, and carefully add them to the oil. Deep-fry until the shrimp are golden brown, about 2½ minutes. Using a wire spider or slotted spoon, transfer the shrimp to the brown-paper-lined baking sheet and keep warm in the oven while frying the remaining shrimp.

4. Serve immediately with the sauce for dipping and the lemon wedges.

155

CRAB CAKES WITH ROASTED JALAPEÑO AIOLI

Tortini di granchio

• •

Beer Pairing: Blonde ale

Makes 4 servings

D: *Crab cakes are a favorite of mine—crunchy on the outside, with creamy crab within. In fact, we purposely make ours on the small side to be sure to have plenty of that golden-brown coating. Gabriele developed the roasted jalapeño aioli just for me because he knows how I like a little extra spice in my sauce.*

1 pound crabmeat, picked over for shells and
   cartilage
½ cup plus ⅓ cup plain dried bread crumbs
1⅓ cup Roasted Jalapeño Aioli (page 158)
1 large egg yolk
1½ tablespoons finely chopped fresh chives

Finely grated zest of ½ orange
⅛ teaspoon sea salt
⅛ teaspoon hot red pepper flakes
Vegetable oil, for frying

Lemon wedges, for serving

1. Mix the crabmeat, ½ cup of the bread crumbs, ⅓ cup of the aioli, the yolk, chives, orange zest, salt, and red pepper flakes in a medium bowl until combined. Shape into 16 plump cakes, each about 1½ inches in diameter. Coat all over with the remaining ⅓ cup bread crumbs, patting to help the crumbs adhere. Transfer to a baking sheet and refrigerate for 15 minutes. (This helps the crab cakes firm up.)

2. Pour enough oil into a very large pan to come ⅛ inch up the sides and heat over medium-high heat until hot but not smoking. In batches without crowding, add the crab cakes and cook, adjusting the heat as needed to keep the crust from browning too fast, until the underside is a deep golden brown, about 3 minutes. Using a metal spatula, flip the crab cakes and cook until the other side is crisp and brown, about 3 minutes more. Transfer to a paper-towel-lined plate to drain briefly.

3. Serve the crab cakes hot, with the lemon wedges and the remaining 1 cup aioli, passed on the side.

MAYONNAISE AND AIOLIS

Maionese e aiolis

• •

Makes about 1¾ cups

America has some great supermarket mayonnaise, but in Italy, it is not uncommon to whip up a batch at home. Homemade mayo in the fridge is a cook's secret weapon, and any sandwich or salad that uses it is elevated a notch or two. It is also a base for garlicky aioli and its variations. With a food processor or even a hand mixer, making it is very easy if you follow a couple of rules. First, be sure the egg or yolks are at room temperature (see Tip, page 97). Also, be sure to add the oil slowly. We've given some time estimates to help you gauge how slow. And use a mix of olive and vegetable oils, because olive oil alone tends to make a very thick mayonnaise that is too heavy to be versatile in all recipes.

1 large egg (or 2 large egg yolks, if using a
    hand mixer), at room temperature
1 tablespoon fresh lemon juice
¼ teaspoon sea salt, plus more for seasoning

Freshly ground black pepper
¾ cup extra-virgin olive oil
¾ cup vegetable or canola oil

1. To make the mayonnaise in food processor: Put the egg, lemon juice, salt, and a few grindings of pepper in a food processor. Mix the olive and vegetable oils together in a liquid measuring cup. With the machine running, very slowly dribble in the oil through the feed tube—it should take at least 1½ minutes to add the oil mixture. The mayonnaise will seem fairly liquid at first, but it will eventually thicken, and you'll hear the motor's noise deepen.

   To make with an electric hand mixer: Beat the egg yolks, lemon juice, salt, and a few grindings of pepper together in a medium bowl with the mixer set at medium speed. Mix the oils together in a liquid measuring cup. A teaspoon at a time, beat the oils into the egg mixture—it should take at least 2 minutes to add the oil mixture.

2. Season the mayonnaise to taste with the salt and pepper. Transfer the mayonnaise to a covered container. (The mayonnaise can be stored in the refrigerator for up to 5 days.)

AIOLI
Add 1 garlic clove, minced, to the food processor with the egg.

ROASTED JALAPEÑO AIOLI
Cut 3 jalapeños (preferably 2 green and 1 red) in half lengthwise and put, cut side down, on a baking sheet. Bake in a preheated 450°F oven until the skins are blackened in spots, about 20 minutes. Let cool completely. Discard the stems, seeds, ribs, and skin. Finely chop the jalapeños. Stir into 1 cup aioli.

SALMON WITH SALSA VERDE

Salmone con salsa verde

· ·

Wine Pairing: Chardonnay or Pinot Grigio
Makes 4 servings

G: *Because salmon is not a Mediterranean fish, I didn't grow up with it, and I have other favorites. But it is always available at our market, so my solution is to trick it into thinking that it is Italian. This bright green condiment (salsa verde means green sauce in Italian as well as Spanish) has such Tuscan favorites as olive oil, capers, anchovies, and garlic blended together with a big handful of parsley leaves to dress up plainly cooked seafood in just a few minutes. Here, we cook the salmon on top of the stove, but try grilled or poached salmon with salsa verde too.*

SALSA VERDE

¾ cup extra-virgin olive oil
⅓ cup coarsely chopped flat-leaf parsley
1 tablespoon drained and rinsed nonpareil capers
2 anchovy fillets in oil, drained and finely chopped
1½ tablespoons fresh lemon juice
1 garlic clove, finely chopped
Sea salt and freshly ground black pepper

1 tablespoon extra-virgin olive oil
4 salmon fillets (about 6 ounces each)
Sea salt and freshly ground black pepper

1. To make the *salsa verde*: Process the oil, parsley, capers, anchovies, lemon juice, and garlic in a food processor or blender until the parsley is minced. Season to taste with the salt and pepper. Transfer to a bowl.

2. Heat the oil in a large nonstick skillet over medium-high heat. Season the salmon to taste with the salt and pepper. Add the salmon, skin side up, and cook until the flesh is lightly browned, about 3 minutes. Flip the salmon and cover the skillet. Cook until the skin is browned and the flesh is rosy pink when pierced in the center with the tip of a small knife, about 3 minutes more.

3. Transfer each fillet to a dinner plate and serve with the *salsa verde* passed on the side.

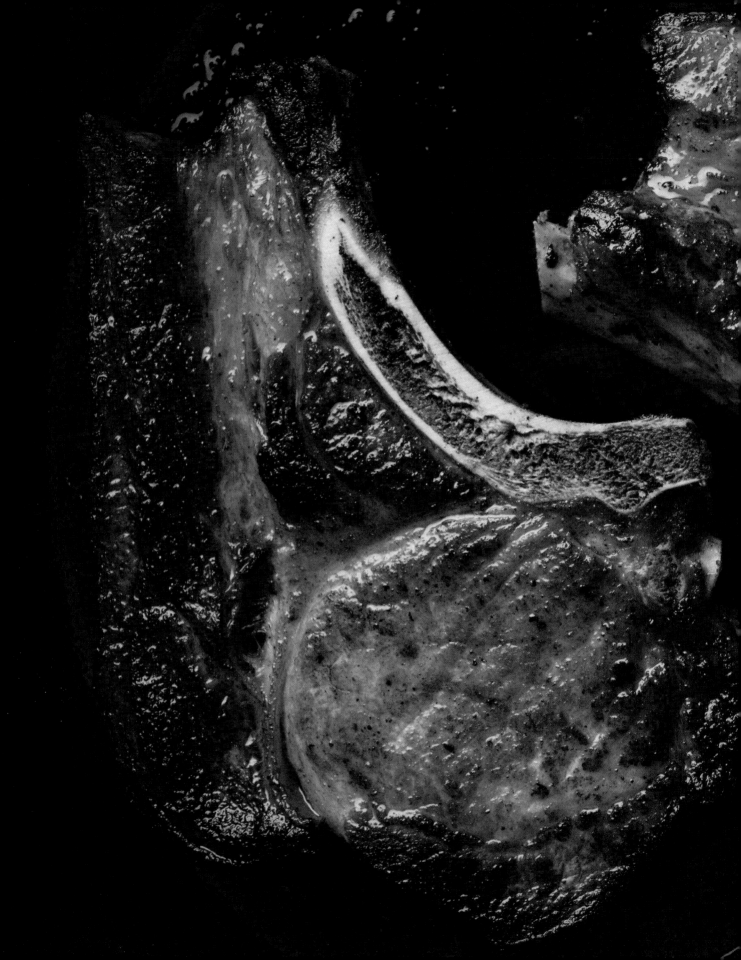

MEAT

ROAST BEEF WITH BABY ONIONS

Rosbif con cipolline

• •

Wine Pairing: Chianti Riserva
Makes 6 to 8 servings

G: *My mom makes roast beef in the classic Tuscan style, rubbed with a simple thyme and rosemary mixture before baking, always served with baby onions on the side. The only change I've made is to roast the baby onions along with the meat so they can pick up the flavor from the pan juices . . . and to satisfy my family's love of roasted vegetables. If you need an impressive beef roast for a special meal, this is the recipe to use.*

Special equipment: kitchen twine

1 boneless rib roast (about 5½ pounds)
1 garlic clove, peeled and cut into about 20 thin slivers, approximately the size of slivered almonds
2 teaspoons extra-virgin olive oil
1½ teaspoons sea salt
½ teaspoon freshly ground black pepper

1 tablespoon plus 1 teaspoon finely chopped fresh rosemary
1 tablespoon plus 1 teaspoon finely chopped fresh thyme
2 pounds small white boiling (pearl or baby) onions, unpeeled
½ cup dry white wine

1. A few hours (or the night) before roasting the beef, trim the top layer of fat so that only a ¼-inch layer remains. Using the tip of a small sharp knife, pierce the beef about 20 times and insert a garlic sliver into each piercing. Rub the beef with a thin layer of oil. Season all over with a mixture of the salt and the pepper. Combine 1 tablespoon each of the rosemary and thyme and rub on the top and bottom exterior of the beef, but not on the cut sides. Tie the roast lengthwise and crosswise with kitchen twine. Place on a plate, cover loosely with plastic wrap, and refrigerate for at least 4 and up to 24 hours. Remove from the refrigerator and let stand at room temperature for 1 hour to lose its chill before roasting.

2. While the roast is standing, prepare the onions: Bring a large saucepan of water to a boil over high heat. Add the onions and boil until the skins loosen, about 1 minute. Drain, rinse under cold water, and drain again. Using a small sharp knife, cut off the top and bottom of each onion, peel the onions, and pierce an X in the top and bottom of the onions. (This helps keep them from splitting when cooked.)

3. Position a rack in the center of the oven and preheat the oven to 350°F.

4. Place the beef, fat side up, in a roasting pan. Roast for 1½ hours. Transfer the roast to a plate and pour off all but 1 tablespoon of the fat in the pan. Add the onions and roll them in the pan to coat

with the fat and pan juices. Move the onions to the sides of the pan and return the beef to the pan. Return to the oven and continue roasting until an instant-read thermometer inserted in the center of the beef reads 125°F for medium rare, about 30 minutes. Place the roast on large platter and let stand for 10 to 15 minutes. If the onions are still firm, increase the oven temperature to 400°F and continue roasting, stirring occasionally, until tender, 5 to 15 minutes depending on their size. Transfer the onions to a bowl and cover with aluminum foil to keep warm.

5. Pour off and discard the fat in the pan, leaving any browned bits on the bottom of the pan, and place it over high heat on the stove. Add the wine and bring to a boil, stirring up the browned bits in the pan with a wooden spoon. Remove from the stove.

6. Discard the twine and carve the roast. Add the glazed onions to the platter, drizzle with the pan sauce, and serve.

BAROLO POT ROAST

Brasato al Barolo

. . . .

Wine Paring: Ideally the same Barolo used in the recipe, or its riserva

Makes 6 to 8 servings

This pot roast will satisfy you right down to the bone. The beef is marinated with red wine and aromatics that also flavor the rich sauce. For the best results, use a full-bodied wine, such as Barolo or Chianti, and try to serve the same with the dish itself. The cinnamon stick is a remnant of the period when Italians used a lot of spices in their cooking, but we consider it entirely optional. Now you have to make a bigger decision: What to serve on the side? We think that you can't do better than plain polenta.

Special equipment: kitchen twine

MARINADE

1 boneless beef chuck roast, cut 2 inches thick (about 3½ pounds)

1 bottle (750 ml) Barolo wine or another hearty red wine

One 3-inch sprig fresh rosemary

One 3-inch cinnamon stick (optional)

1 bay leaf

1 teaspoon sea salt, plus more for seasoning

½ teaspoon freshly ground black pepper, plus more for seasoning

2 tablespoons extra-virgin olive oil, plus more as needed

1 large red onion, coarsely chopped

2 medium celery ribs, coarsely chopped

2 medium carrots, coarsely chopped

3 garlic cloves, crushed

4 cups Vegetable Broth (page 67), plus more as needed

Coarsely torn fresh flat-leaf parsley leaves, for garnish

1. To marinate the beef: The day (or at least a few hours) before cooking, tie the beef crosswise in a few places with kitchen twine. Mix the wine, rosemary, cinnamon, if using, and bay leaf in a large bowl. Add the beef and put a plate on top to submerge in the marinade. Refrigerate, occasionally turning the beef, at least 4 hours or overnight.

2. Position a rack in the lower third of the oven and preheat the oven to 300°F.

3. Strain the beef and the marinade in a colander over a bowl, reserving the marinade and its solids. Pat the beef as dry as possible with paper towels. Sprinkle with 1 teaspoon of the salt and ½ teaspoon of the pepper.

4. Heat the oil in a large Dutch oven over medium-high heat until the oil is very hot but not smoking. Add the beef and cook, turning occasionally, until well seared and browned all over, about 15 minutes. Transfer the beef to a plate. Add more oil to the Dutch oven, if needed. Add the onion, celery, carrot, and garlic and cover. Cook, stirring often, until tender, about 6 minutes. Season to taste with the salt and pepper.

5. Add ½ cup of the strained marinade and bring to a boil, scraping up the browned bits with a wooden spoon. Add the remaining marinade, including the cinnamon, rosemary, and bay leaf, and bring to a boil. Return the beef and any juices on the plate to the Dutch oven. Pour in enough vegetable broth to almost cover the beef. If you run out of broth, use water. Bring to a simmer.

6. Cover the pot with aluminum foil (this helps with cleanup later) and then its lid. Bake, turning the roast halfway during cooking, until it is fork-tender, about 3 hours.

7. Transfer the beef to a deep serving platter and tent it with aluminum foil. Remove the cinnamon stick, rosemary sprig, and bay leaf from the cooking liquid. Skim off any fat that rises to the surface of the liquid. Bring the cooking liquid with the vegetables to a boil over high heat and cook, stirring often, until reduced by about half, about 15 minutes. Using an immersion blender, puree the mixture in the pot. (Or, in batches, puree the mixture in a blender, making sure to leave the lid ajar to release the steam.) Season to taste with the salt and pepper.

8. Discard the strings from the beef. Cut the beef crosswise into ½-inch-thick slices and arrange them on the platter. Cover the beef with some of the sauce and transfer the remaining sauce to a sauceboat. Sprinkle the pot roast with the torn parsley leaves and serve hot with the sauce on the side.

STEAK PIZZAIOLA

Cotolette alla pizzaiola

• • • • • • • • • • • • • • • • • • • •

Wine Pairing: Young Sangiovese
Makes 4 servings

G: *If you assume that an Italian elementary school lunchroom would serve pretty good food, you would be right. I haven't had a lot of American cafeteria fare, so I can't compare. But I will say that I have great memories of this dish with cheap round steaks smothered in tomato sauce topped with melted mozzarella cheese. All kids love that "pizza-y" combination, and my schoolmates and I would make each tray disappear. There are more than a few adults that find this dish irresistible too . . . like me. I am not a big oregano fan, but if you wish, substitute it for the basil, because for some people, it isn't "pizza" unless it has that herb.*

RED SAUCE WITH ANCHOVIES AND CAPERS
2 tablespoons extra-virgin olive oil
1 small red onion (about 1 cup chopped)
2 anchovy fillets in olive oil, drained and finely
    chopped
3 garlic cloves, minced
¼ teaspoon hot red pepper flakes
One 28-ounce can whole peeled tomatoes in
    juice, pureed in a blender
2 tablespoons drained and rinsed nonpareil
    capers
2 tablespoons finely chopped fresh basil leaves,
    plus more for serving
Sea salt and freshly ground black pepper

STEAK
4 bottom round steaks, cut ½ inch thick (about
    8 ounces each)
Sea salt and freshly ground black pepper
2 tablespoons extra-virgin olive oil, plus more
    as needed
8 ounces fresh mozzarella, coarsely shredded
    (about 2 cups, see Tip, page 169)

1. To make the sauce: Heat the oil in a medium saucepan over medium heat. Add the onion and anchovies and cook, stirring occasionally, until the onion is tender, about 4 minutes. Stir in the garlic and red pepper flakes and cook until the garlic is fragrant, about 1 minute. Stir in the tomatoes and ½ cup water. Bring to a simmer and reduce the heat to medium low. Simmer, stirring occasionally, until the sauce has reduced slightly but is still fairly liquid, about 20 minutes. (The sauce will reduce more when cooked with the steaks, so no need to cook it more at this point.) Stir in the capers and basil. Season to taste with the salt and pepper. Remove from heat and set the sauce aside.

2. To prepare the steaks: Cut the steak into 8 equal pieces. Using a pointed meat mallet, pound each steak well on both sides to tenderize them. If needed, cut the steaks in half vertically to fit the skillet. Season all over with the salt and pepper.

3. Heat the oil in a very large (at least 12 inches in diameter) skillet over medium-high heat until it is hot but not smoking. In batches without crowding, add the steak and cook, turning halfway during cooking, until seared on both sides, 2 to 3 minutes. Transfer to a platter.

4. Add the sauce and bring to a simmer, scraping up the browned bits in the skillet with a wooden spoon. Return all of the steaks to the skillet and submerge them in the sauce. Bring to a simmer and reduce the heat to low. Cover the skillet and simmer, occasionally turning the steaks, until they are tender, about 50 minutes. If the sauce thickens too much, stir in $\frac{1}{4}$ cup water.

5. Move the steaks in the sauce so they form two layers. Sprinkle with half of the cheese to cover the top layer. Cover with the lid and cook until the mozzarella melts, about 1 minute. Transfer the cheese-topped steaks to a platter. Repeat with the remaining steaks in the skillet and the rest of the mozzarella. Spoon the sauce in the pan around the steaks, sprinkle with the additional basil, and serve.

TIP To shred fresh mozzarella, which is much softer than the industrial low-moisture variety, freeze the cheese for an hour or so to firm it.

MEATBALLS WITH TOMATO-MINT SAUCE

Polpettine con salsa alla menta

● ●

Wine Pairing: Ideally the same Chianti used in the recipe, or its riserva
Makes 4 to 6 servings

We eat meatballs in the Tuscan manner, without pasta. We'll put out a platter of them, and before long, they disappear. In this recipe, we use both lamb and beef, but they are also very good when made with one or the other. One tip about buying ground lamb, however: It can be quite fatty, so if possible, have the butcher grind well-trimmed lamb shoulder for you. Couscous would be a good side dish or just serve them with lots of crusty bread for wiping up the sauce. Mint may be a surprising addition, but it really adds a fresh flavor.

TOMATO-MINT SAUCE

2 tablespoons extra-virgin olive oil
1 small red onion, chopped
2 garlic cloves, minced
1 cup hearty red wine, such as Chianti
One 28-ounce can whole peeled tomatoes in juice, pureed in a blender
2 tablespoons finely chopped fresh mint, plus more for serving
Sea salt and freshly ground black pepper

MEATBALLS

1 pound ground round beef (15 percent fat)
1 pound lean ground lamb
½ cup plain dried bread crumbs
1 medium yellow onion, very finely chopped
2 garlic cloves, minced
2 tablespoons finely chopped fresh flat-leaf parsley
2 tablespoons finely chopped fresh mint
2 tablespoons freshly grated Pecorino Romano cheese, plus more for serving
2 large egg yolks
1½ teaspoons sea salt
½ teaspoon freshly ground black pepper
¼ cup extra-virgin olive oil, plus more as needed

1. To make the sauce: Heat the oil in a medium saucepan over medium heat. Add the red onion and garlic and cook, stirring occasionally, until the onion is translucent, about 4 minutes. Add the wine and bring to a boil. Stir in the pureed tomatoes, 1 cup water, and mint and bring to a boil. Reduce the heat to low and simmer, stirring occasionally, to blend the flavors, about 20 minutes. The sauce should remain somewhat liquid as it will reduce more when cooked with the meatballs and the additional sauce will distribute the heat and encourage even cooking. Season to taste with the salt and pepper. Remove from the heat.

2. Meanwhile, make the meatballs: Using clean hands, mix the ground beef, lamb, bread crumbs, yellow onion, garlic, parsley, mint, Pecorino, yolks, salt, and pepper in a large bowl. Using about a tablespoon for each, roll the mixture into 36 meatballs and transfer the balls to a baking sheet.

3. Heat the oil in a very large skillet over medium-high heat. In batches without crowding, add the meatballs and cook, turning occasionally, until browned all over, about 6 minutes, adding oil as needed. Using a slotted spoon, transfer the meatballs to a platter. Pour out the fat in the pan.

4. Add the sauce to the skillet and bring to a simmer, scraping up the browned bits with a wooden spoon. Return the meatballs to the sauce and reduce the heat to low. Partially cover the skillet and cook, occasionally stirring the sauce, until the meatballs are tender, about 30 minutes. If the sauce is reduced too much, stir in enough water to loosen it. Transfer the meatballs and the sauce to a deep platter. Serve hot, with the Pecorino on the side.

VEAL WITH LEMON SAUCE

Scaloppine di vitella al limone

· ·

Wine Pairing: Verdicchio

Makes 4 to 6 servings

Veal has a very delicate flavor, so we prefer it simply cooked so it can shine. At least, that is our opinion—let other people carry on about breaded, fried, sauced, and mozzarella-ed veal Parmigiano. This is one of our very favorites, with a pleasantly tart wine and lemon sauce. Whenever this is on the dinner table, our kids devour it. For side dishes, go with plain steamed asparagus spears and mashed potatoes (page 222).

1½ pounds veal scaloppine
Sea salt and freshly ground black pepper
2 tablespoons extra-virgin olive oil, plus more as needed

⅓ cup (45 grams) unbleached all-purpose flour
¾ cup dry white wine, such as Pinot Grigio
3 tablespoons fresh lemon juice

1. Pound the veal with a flat meat mallet between two plastic bags until less than ¼ inch thick. Cut the veal into 12 to 18 pieces, as equal in size as possible. Season the veal with the salt and pepper.

2. Heat the oil in a very large skillet over medium-high heat until the oil is hot but not smoking. Spread the flour in a shallow bowl. In batches without crowding, dredge the veal in the flour, shake off the excess, and immediately add the veal to the skillet. (Do not try to save time by flouring all of the veal at once, as the coating will get gummy and affect the texture of the finished dish.) Cook until the underside is lightly browned, about 1½ minutes. Cook to brown the other side, about 1½ minutes more. Transfer the veal to a platter and tent with aluminum foil to keep warm. If the oil burns, discard it, wipe out the skillet with paper towels, and return the skillet to medium-high heat. Add more oil to the skillet as needed.

3. Add the wine and lemon juice to the skillet and bring to a boil, scraping up the browned bits in the pan with a wooden spoon. Return the veal and any juices to the skillet and cook, turning the pieces over in the sauce with tongs, just until the sauce is thickened and the veal is hot, about 1 minute. Season the sauce with salt and pepper. Transfer the veal and sauce to dinner plates and serve.

BRINED PORK CHOPS WITH SAGE-ALMOND PESTO

Bistecchina di maiale con pesto di salvia

● ●

Makes 4 servings

G: Pesto alla genovese, *made with basil and pine nuts, is the original pesto, and it is justly famous. I am nothing if not a traditionalist when it comes to Italian cooking, so any variations have to be justified and make sense to me before I will give them any credence. This pesto, with parsley, sage, and almonds, is worthy and goes a long way to dress up simple meats like these pork chops. Brining is another American cooking technique that I came to appreciate very slowly, but I will selectively use it on lean cuts of meat (like pork chops) and whole chicken (see page 191), where it does help keep them moist after cooking.*

BRINED PORK CHOPS
⅓ cup plus 1 tablespoon sea salt
½ cup sugar
½ cup packed coarsely chopped fresh sage
  stems (keep sage leaves for pesto)
1 teaspoon black peppercorns
2 cups chilled dry white wine, such as Pinot
  Grigio
2 cups iced water
4 center-cut bone-in loin pork chops (about
  8 ounces each)

SAGE-ALMOND PESTO
1 garlic clove, crushed
1 cup loosely packed fresh flat-leaf parsley leaves
⅓ cup sliced natural almonds, toasted
½ cup freshly grated Parmigiano-Reggiano cheese
¼ cup loosely packed fresh sage leaves
Finely grated zest of ½ lemon
Pinch of hot red pepper flakes
½ cup extra-virgin olive oil
1 tablespoon fresh lemon juice
Sea salt and freshly ground black pepper
1 tablespoon extra-virgin olive oil

1. To make the brined pork chops: Bring 1 quart water, the salt, sugar, sage stems, and peppercorns to a boil in a medium saucepan over high heat, stirring to dissolve the salt and sugar. Pour the mixture into a large bowl. Add the wine and iced water and stir until the ice is melted and the brine is chilled. Add the pork chops and cover. Refrigerate for 2 to 3 hours, no longer.

2. Meanwhile, to make the pesto: With the food processor running, drop the garlic through the machine's tube. Add the parsley, almonds, Parmigiano, sage leaves, lemon zest, and red pepper flakes, and process until very finely chopped. With the machine running, gradually pour in the oil, followed by the lemon juice. Season to taste with the salt and pepper. Transfer to a small bowl.

3. Drain the pork chops and pat them dry with paper towels. Heat the oil in a very large skillet over medium-high heat. Add the pork chops and cook until the underside is browned, about 3 minutes. Flip the chops and cover the skillet. Reduce the heat to medium. Cook, covered, until the pork shows no sign of pink when pierced at the bone, about 10 minutes more. Transfer the chops to dinner plates. Top each with a dollop of pesto and serve. (The remaining pesto can be covered with a thin layer of olive oil, covered, and refrigerated for up to 5 days. Serve at room temperature.)

PORK CHOPS WITH BLACK KALE

Bistecchina di maiale col cavolo nero

....

Makes 4 servings

When autumn rolls around, it is time to put away the grill and cook up a skillet of these tasty pork chops, served on black kale (called cavolo nero *in Tuscany). This crinkly gray, dark-green variety is used in soups, side dishes, and can even be served as a main course on a bed of polenta. To a Tuscan, the appearance of kale signals the beginning of the cold weather season, as it is one of those vegetables that tastes better and is more tender after being "kissed by the frost." In fact, at the farm, we do not harvest* cavolo nero *until deep into the season, when it has grown about two feet tall. It is much tougher than the American version, which is one reason why Italian recipes always simmer the leaves for a long time in liquid.*

BLACK KALE

1 pound black (also called lacinato, Tuscan, or dinosaur) kale, thick stems removed, leaves coarsely chopped

2 tablespoons extra-virgin olive oil

½ cup (¼-inch) diced guanciale or pancetta

1 garlic clove, chopped

Pinch of hot red pepper flakes

Sea salt

PORK CHOPS

4 center-cut, bone-in pork loin chops (about 8 ounces each)

Sea salt and freshly ground black pepper

2 tablespoons extra-virgin olive oil

⅔ cup dry white wine

4 pieces Tuscan Country Toast (page 59), with or without garlic, for serving

1. To make the kale: Bring a medium saucepan of salted water to a boil over high heat. Add the kale and cook until just tender, about 5 minutes. Drain well and rinse under cold running water. Drain again. A handful at a time, squeeze the excess water from the kale.

2. Heat the oil in a medium skillet over medium-high heat. Add the guanciale and cook until it begins to crisp, about 2 minutes. Stir in the garlic and cook just until it turns golden, about 30 seconds. Add the red pepper flakes, followed by the kale. Cook, stirring occasionally, until the kale is heated through, about 2 minutes. Remove from the heat. Season to taste with the salt.

3. To make the pork chops: Season the pork chops with the salt and pepper. Heat the oil in a very large skillet over medium heat until it is hot but not smoking. Add the pork chops and cook, turning halfway through cooking, until browned on both sides, about 8 minutes. Transfer to a platter.

4. Pour out the excess fat in the skillet. Add the wine and bring to a simmer, stirring up the browned bits in the skillet. Cook until the wine reduces slightly, about 1 minute. Return the chops to the skillet and cook, turning constantly, until they show no sign of pink when pierced to the bone, about 3 minutes.

5. For each serving, place a *fettunta* on a dinner plate. Top with an equal amount of the kale, followed by a pork chop. Drizzle with the pan juices and serve immediately.

AUNT LAURA'S PORK ROLLS

Involtini di maiale

•••••••••••••••••••••••••••••••••

Wine Pairing: Trebbiano from Frascati
Makes 4 servings

G: *My Aunt Laura would make these rolls for family dinners, and they are simple enough for a week-night meal but special enough for a party. (I know because after the last time I cooked them, Debi served the leftovers to her girlfriends and they ate every morsel.) The trick is getting the right cut of pork cutlet, which, like veal scaloppine, should be from the leg. Most American supermarkets have boneless pork loin cutlets, which are leaner. You can use them if you pound them into large pieces about 3 inches square, and only cook them for 10 minutes to avoid drying them out.*

Special equipment: wooden toothpicks

8 boneless pork cutlets (scaloppine) cut from the leg (about 3 ounces each)

8 slices Emmentaler or Gruyère cheese, each about 3 inches square

16 thin slices capocollo (see Note)

8 fresh sage leaves

Sea salt and freshly ground black pepper

3 tablespoons extra-virgin olive oil

½ cup dry white wine

1. Top each pork cutlet with the cheese, broken up to be rolled in the cutlet, 2 slices of capocollo, and 1 sage leaf. Starting at a long end, fold in the short ends about ½ inch, then roll up the cutlet to enclose the filling, and fasten it closed lengthwise with a wooden toothpick. Season with the salt and pepper.

2. Heat the oil in a very large skillet over medium heat. Add the rolls and cover. Cook, occasionally turning the rolls, until they are nicely browned and tender when pierced with the top of a small sharp knife, about 20 minutes. Transfer the rolls to a platter and tent them with aluminum foil to keep warm.

3. Return the skillet to high heat. Add the wine and bring to a boil, scraping up the browned bits in the skillet with a wooden spoon. Cook, stirring occasionally, until the sauce is reduced by about one-third, 3 to 5 minutes. Remove any pieces of cheese that escaped from the rolls. Pour the sauce over the pork rolls. Let the rolls stand in the sauce for a minute or so, and serve.

NOTE Capocollo (also called *capicola* or *coppa*) is a dry-cured salame made from a single muscle that runs from the neck to the pork shoulder. It is mildly spiced, dry-cured, and one of the very best of all Italian cold cuts.

ROASTED SPARERIBS WITH TOMATO-WINE SAUCE

Rosticciana alla cacciatora

• •

Wine Pairing: Super Tuscan red wine from Siena or Bolgheri

Makes 6 to 8 servings

Our family likes barbecued ribs as much as anyone. We insist that you try these Italian baby backs. They are not cooked outside, but roasted in the oven with lots of herbs in a no-fuss tomato sauce. (Use either red or white wine for the sauce, but we have a preference toward red to give the sauce a deeper color.) While the tender, juicy ribs are the stars here, the sauce gives it a run for its money, so be sure to serve polenta or pasta too. And put out plenty of napkins, because like American ribs, these are impossible to eat without a lot of finger licking.

HERB PASTE
- ⅓ cup extra-virgin olive oil
- 2 tablespoons finely chopped fresh rosemary
- 2 tablespoons finely chopped fresh flat-leaf parsley
- 1 tablespoon finely chopped fresh mint (if you have it, substitute 1½ teaspoons *nipitella* for half of the mint)
- 2 teaspoons finely chopped fresh lavender flowers or 1 teaspoon dried lavender (optional)
- 1 tablespoon sea salt
- 2 teaspoons freshly ground black pepper

- 2 racks baby back pork ribs (about 6½ pounds total)
- 4 tablespoons extra-virgin olive oil, plus more as needed
- 3 garlic cloves, coarsely chopped
- ¼ teaspoon hot red pepper flakes
- 1 cup dry white wine or hearty red wine
- One 28-ounce can whole peeled tomatoes in juice, pureed in a blender
- ¾ cup pitted and coarsely chopped oil-brined black olives
- Sea salt and freshly ground black pepper
- Fresh flat-leaf parsley, for serving

1. To make the herb paste: Puree the oil, rosemary, parsley, mint, lavender, salt, and pepper in a mini food processor or blender into a wet paste.

2. Cut the ribs in half vertically to make 4 slabs. Slather and rub the herb mixture all over the ribs.

3. Heat 2 tablespoons of the oil in a large, deep skillet over medium-high heat. In batches, add the ribs, meaty side down, and cook until the underside is browned, about 4 minutes. Turn and brown the other side (which won't turn brown all over, only on the edges that touch the pan), about 3 minutes. Transfer the ribs, bone side up, to a very large metal roasting pan.

4. Meanwhile, position a rack in the center of the oven and preheat the oven to 400°F.

5. Pour out the fat from the skillet. Add the remaining 2 tablespoons oil and let the skillet cool for a few minutes. (The pan is piping hot, and if you add the garlic immediately, it could burn.) Add

the garlic and red pepper flakes and cook over low heat until fragrant, about 1 minute. Increase the heat to medium and add the wine, using a wooden spoon to stir up the browned bits in the skillet. Bring to a boil and cook until reduced by half, about 3 minutes. Stir in the tomatoes and boil until slightly thickened, about 3 minutes. Pour over the ribs and spread so the sauce runs into the bottom of the pan. Bring to a simmer over medium heat. Cover tightly with aluminum foil.

6. Roast for 15 minutes. Reduce the heat to 350°F and bake until the ribs are very tender and the meat has pulled about ½ inch from the ends of the bones, about 45 minutes. Transfer the ribs to a carving board and tent with aluminum foil to keep warm.

7. Let the sauce stand and skim some of the fat off the surface of the sauce. Add the olives and bring to a boil over high heat, stirring often. Boil until the sauce is slightly reduced, about 3 minutes. Season to taste with the salt and pepper.

8. Using kitchen shears or a large knife, cut between the bones. Transfer the individual ribs to a deep serving platter and pour the sauce on top. Sprinkle with the parsley and serve.

TIP We sometimes make this dish for the sole purpose of turning it into an incredible pasta sauce. In this case use one large slab of ribs (about 3 pounds) with half the amount of herb rub. When the ribs are cooked and tender, remove from the sauce, let them cool until easier to handle, and cut the meat off the bones. Chop the meat into fairly small pieces (about the size of a dime), and stir into the sauce. This is especially good with sturdy or tube-shaped pasta like ziti or rigatoni.

MARINATED LAMB SAUTÉ WITH CUCUMBER-YOGURT SAUCE

Agnello alla saracena

••

Wine Pairing: Rosso di Montalcino

Makes 4 servings

The Italian name for this dish is agnello alla saracena *(Saracen-style lamb), dubbed after the Muslims who invaded Italy in the Byzantine period and left behind many culinary influences. You'll find similar sautés all over the country because boneless leg of lamb is not only fairly plentiful and flavorful, but also very quick to cook. Don't over-marinate the lamb, or it will get a soft texture. Serve this with the Couscous with Cherry Tomatoes and Olives (page 223).*

CUCUMBER-YOGURT SAUCE
1 Israeli (or Persian) cucumber, thinly sliced
   crosswise
½ teaspoon sea salt, plus more for seasoning
½ cup plain low-fat Greek yogurt
1 tablespoon finely chopped fresh cilantro
2 teaspoons finely chopped fresh mint
Freshly ground black pepper

LAMB
2 tablespoons fresh lemon juice
1 tablespoon white wine vinegar
2 garlic cloves, crushed
½ teaspoon sea salt
¼ teaspoon freshly ground black pepper
4 tablespoons extra-virgin olive oil
1½ pounds boneless leg of lamb, well trimmed
   and cut into ¾-inch cubes

1. To make the sauce: Mix the cucumber slices and ½ teaspoon of the salt in a colander. Let stand on a plate to drain for 30 minutes to 1 hour. Pat the cucumber dry with paper towels. Mix the yogurt, cilantro, and mint in a small bowl and stir in the cucumber. Season to taste with salt and pepper. Cover and refrigerate for up to 4 hours. Remove from the refrigerator about 30 minutes before serving to lose its chill.

2. To prepare the lamb: Whisk the lemon juice, vinegar, garlic, and salt and pepper in a medium glass or ceramic bowl. Gradually whisk in 3 tablespoons of the oil. Add the lamb and mix well. Cover and refrigerate, stirring occasionally, for about 1 hour.

3. Drain the lamb well, discarding the marinade. Heat the remaining 1 tablespoon oil in a very large skillet over high heat until it is hot but not smoking. Add the lamb and let cook without stirring until the bottom side is seared and beginning to brown, about 2 minutes. Flip the lamb over and cook, stirring occasionally, until seared on all sides, about 4 minutes more for medium-rare lamb. Serve the lamb immediately with the sauce passed on the side.

ROAST LEG OF LAMB WITH GARLIC AND ROSEMARY

Cosciotto di agnello arrosto con aglio e rosmarino

• •

Wine Pairing: Vino Nobile di Montepulciano
Makes 6 servings

There are few cuts of meat more majestic than a whole leg of lamb. It is right up there with the roast beef on page 163 as a main course for a holiday meal (we're thinking Easter in this case, a big holiday in Tuscany). We prefer the classic lamb seasonings of garlic and rosemary, spiked with some lemon zest and juice. Simple and elegant, serve it with the Pan-Roasted Green Beans and Golden Roasted Potatoes (pages 208 and 216).

5 garlic cloves, crushed
2 teaspoons sea salt
¼ cup coarsely chopped fresh rosemary
Finely grated zest of 1 lemon
3 tablespoons extra-virgin olive oil
3 tablespoons fresh lemon juice

1½ teaspoons freshly ground black pepper
1 semi-boneless leg of lamb, with leg bone
    (about 7 pounds)
1 lemon, cut into thin rounds, for garnish
Fresh rosemary sprigs, for garnish

1. At least 4 hours (or the night) before cooking, marinate the lamb. Coarsely chop the crushed garlic on a cutting board. Sprinkle with the salt and chop and smear the garlic into a coarse paste. Add the rosemary and lemon zest and continue chopping and scraping until well combined. Transfer to a small bowl and stir in the oil, lemon juice, and pepper to make a thin paste. (Or puree all of the ingredients in a mini food processor.)

2. Place the lamb on a large rimmed baking sheet. Using the tip of a small sharp knife, pierce the lamb about 15 times, making slits about 1 inch wide and deep all over the lamb. Using a small spoon and your fingertip, fill each piercing with some of the rosemary paste. Slather the remaining rosemary paste all over the lamb. Cover with plastic wrap and refrigerate for at least 4 hours or overnight. Remove from the refrigerator and let stand at room temperature for 1 hour to remove its chill before cooking.

3. Position a rack in the bottom third of the oven and preheat the oven to 400°F. Place the lamb in a large roasting pan. Roast the lamb for 15 minutes. Reduce the oven temperature to 350°F. Continue roasting until an instant-read thermometer inserted in the thickest part of the lamb not touching a bone reads 130°F for medium rare, about 1¼ hours. During the last 20 minutes of roasting, arrange the lemon slices on top of the lamb.

4. Transfer the lamb to a carving board and let rest for 10 to 15 minutes. Set the lemon slices aside. Using the leg bone as a handle, carve the lamb: Slice vertically along the roast in the boneless area, then parallel to the bone in the shank section. Transfer the slices to a platter and pour the carving juices on top. Garnish with the rosemary sprigs and lemon slices and serve.

OUR NEIGHBORHOOD

Our neighborhood is extraordinary, even by New York's standards. Windsor Terrace is only a few blocks wide and long, and is shaped like an angular comma. Its shopping street is Prospect Park West, even though it doesn't run along the park at all and really should be called 9th Avenue.

We like to shop every day for our groceries, which ensures fresh ingredients for our cooking. It's easy to stock up on produce, and then forget what is hidden in the back of the fridge. We find that with daily shopping, we don't have as much food going bad, and this reduces waste.

Having a single street with all of our essential stores within strolling distance of each other is, in our opinion, the perfect way to shop. In close proximity, we have our produce stand, butcher, grocery store, wine shop, and pharmacy. We also have an independent bookstore and a small bakery. Just off the main street is a wonderful antiques shop where we have found some of our favorite treasures. On one corner stands an iconic blue-collar hangout, Farrell's Bar & Grill. Farrell's did not serve women until 1972 and gained extra notoriety when Shirley MacLaine staged a protest "drink-in."

United Meat Market is a business that personifies the uniqueness of Windsor Terrace. Not many neighborhoods in any city still have a butcher store. When we lived in Los Angeles, Gabriele constantly bemoaned the plastic-wrapped, precut meats in the antiseptic supermarkets. (Debi remembers the local market in Fiesole, where you can buy everything from fried pig liver to bras.) So, to have an old-school butcher within walking distance of our house is heaven.

The current owners, brothers Rocco and Joe Gallo, have run the store since 1987, and there has been a butcher in the building since the fifties. Of course, the mainstay of the business is their beautifully prepared meats. Often, when Gabriele shops for the family, steaks are individually cut to order

from a larger roast. In addition to the range of meat and poultry, the brothers also sell groceries from their native Italy, and some house-made specialty items like *arancini* (rice balls) and pasta sauces. Customers may come in for a steak and leave with more food and some cooking advice too. Their mozzarella is made twice (!) daily.

Our largest farmer's market is a few blocks away in Grand Army Plaza. On Saturdays, we will take the car to buy the very freshest fruits and vegetables of the season, and treat ourselves to some other foods (farm-made cheese, freshly baked pastries, local honey) too. In California, we could shop year-round at our local farmer's markets, but on the East Coast, they slow down during the winter months, and we always miss the vendors during the hiatus.

We encourage you to explore your neighborhood and see what kind of shopping treasures might be around, especially when it comes to ethnic grocers. It may take a little thinking outside of the box or an extra few minutes' drive in the car, but there may be something very special in your own backyard.

POULTRY

TUSCAN FRIED CHICKEN

Pollo fritto alla casalinga

• •

Beer Pairing: IPA or English-style pale ale

Makes 4 servings

G: *Fried chicken is another one of those dishes that show up in every cuisine, and Tuscany is no exception. This is a recipe that originated with the Italian Jews in the ghettos of Florence and Rome. I imagine that it was especially popular during Hanukkah when fried foods are traditionally served. Nonetheless, I didn't think much about fried chicken as a kid, even with a Jewish dad; it was the American version that made me a fan. But as much as I like Southern fried chicken, this recipe is a keeper.*

D: *If this doesn't become your go-to recipe for fried chicken, I'd be very surprised. The chicken is marinated in classic Italian flavors of lemon, garlic, and herbs, and then dipped and fried to golden brown. Try to enjoy the chicken soon within a couple of hours of cooking, as it is not nearly as good after it has been refrigerated.*

1 chicken, cut into 8 serving pieces (about 3½ pounds)	¾ teaspoon freshly ground black pepper
¼ cup fresh lemon juice	½ teaspoon hot red pepper flakes
1 tablespoon finely chopped fresh rosemary	3 large eggs
1 tablespoon finely chopped fresh thyme	1 cup (140 grams) unbleached all-purpose flour
2 garlic cloves, minced	Canola oil, for deep-frying
1½ teaspoons sea salt	Lemon wedges, for serving

1. Using a cleaver or large knife, cut each chicken breast half crosswise into two equal pieces to make four breast pieces and 10 pieces of cut-up chicken total. You can also have the butcher do this for you (see Note, page 190).

2. Whisk the lemon juice, rosemary, thyme, garlic, 1 teaspoon of the salt, ½ teaspoon of the pepper, and the red pepper flakes in a large nonreactive bowl. Add the chicken and mix well. Cover and refrigerate, stirring occasionally, for at least 1 but no longer than 2 hours.

3. Set yourself up to coat the chicken. Drain the chicken, leaving any solids clinging to the pieces. Beat the eggs in a shallow bowl. Mix the flour, the remaining ½ teaspoon salt and ¼ teaspoon pepper in a second shallow bowl. Place a large baking sheet near the setup. One at a time, dip the chicken in the eggs, roll in the flour mixture to coat completely, and place on the baking sheet. Let the chicken stand at room temperature while heating the oil.

4. Place a wire rack over a large rimmed baking sheet. Pour enough oil to come about halfway up the sides of a large saucepan and heat over high heat until it registers 350°F on a deep-frying ther-

mometer. (Low-tech tip: If you stick the handle of a wooden spoon in the oil, bubbles will immediately form around the handle.) Using kitchen tongs, carefully add the chicken breast pieces only to the hot oil and cover the saucepan, deep-frying for 4 minutes, or until the underside of the chicken is golden brown. Turn the chicken and leave the pot uncovered. Continue frying until the chicken is completely golden brown and an instant-read thermometer inserted in the thickest part of the chicken reads 165°F, about 3 minutes more. (Remove the chicken from the oil when you take its temperature, or the juices could make the oil splatter.) Transfer the chicken breast pieces to the wire rack. Repeat with the dark meat, cooking for 4 minutes covered, followed by 4 to 6 minutes uncovered, until the chicken is golden brown and the thermometer reads 165°F in the thigh. Transfer the dark meat to the rack and let cool for 5 minutes before serving. Serve warm or at room temperature, with the lemon wedges.

NOTE We cut the chicken breast halves in half again to make a total of 4 smaller pieces. This is because today's chickens are very top heavy, and the whole halves are not easy to cook evenly. Also, a chicken breast as a serving portion is not equal to a drumstick, which has much less meat, and cutting the breast into smaller pieces levels the field.

ROAST CHICKEN ALLA CONTADINA

Pollo arrosto alla contadina

● ●

Wine/Beer Pairing: Young Sangiovese or English-style IPA
Makes 4 to 6 servings

G: *Your search for the perfect, golden roast chicken has ended.* Contadina *means "country style" in Italian, which generally means "farm-fresh ingredients, simply cooked." According to that description, about* all *of our home cooking is* alla contadina! *In Italy, we would not brine the chicken. We raise most of our chickens or buy them from nearby farmers, and they have very diverse diets that give them extra flavor. American supermarket chickens benefit from a moisturizing soak before roasting, and brining seasons them from the inside out too. Other root vegetables, such as turnips or parsnips, can be added or swapped for the carrots.*

BRINE
1 quart hot water
½ cup sea salt
½ cup sugar
1 quart iced water

CHICKEN AND VEGETABLES
1 whole chicken (about 5½ pounds)
2 tablespoons extra-virgin olive oil
Freshly ground black pepper
4 garlic cloves, unpeeled and crushed
4 large Yukon Gold potatoes, cut into ½-inch
    wedges (about 1½ pounds)
6 large carrots, cut into 1-inch chunks (about
    1 pound)
Three 3-inch sprigs of fresh rosemary
Three 3-inch sprigs of fresh thyme
Sea salt

1. To make the brine: Whisk the hot water, salt, and sugar in a tall container (about 4 quarts) or large deep bowl until the salt and sugar are dissolved. Add the iced water and stir until the ice is almost all melted.

2. To brine the chicken: Pull out any yellow fat from the tail area of the chicken and discard with the giblets. Submerge the chicken, breast side down, in the brine. Refrigerate for at least 2 hours and up to 6 hours, no longer.

3. To roast the chicken and vegetables: Position a rack in the center of the oven and preheat the oven to 425°F. The high oven temperature is one of this recipe's secrets.

4. Drain the chicken and pat it dry with paper towels. Rub the chicken skin all over with 1 table-spoon of the olive oil. Season the chicken with pepper, but do not salt it. Put the garlic in the chicken's body cavity. Place the chicken, back side up, on a roasting rack inside a large roasting

pan. (Roasting the chicken for a time with its back up helps brown the underside of the bird and keeps the breast from cooking too quickly and drying out.) Roast for 40 minutes.

5. Insert a wooden spoon in the body cavity to help turn the chicken over, breast side up, letting any juices from the cavity run into the pan. Remove the spoon and roast for 15 minutes. Toss the potatoes, carrots, rosemary, and thyme with the remaining 1 tablespoon oil in a medium bowl. Season to taste with pepper, but not salt, as the pan juices will be salty. Spread the vegetable mixture around the chicken and stir to coat with the pan juices. Continue roasting until an instant-read thermometer inserted in the thickest part of the breast, not touching a bone, reads 165°F, about 45 minutes.

6. Insert the wooden spoon into the body cavity, and tilt the chicken so its juices run into the roasting pan. Transfer the chicken to a large, deep platter and let stand for 10 minutes. Spread out the vegetables and continue roasting them while the chicken stands until they are browned and tender, about 10 minutes. (If the chicken and vegetables are done at the same time . . . you rock! If they are, keep them warm in the turned-off oven with its door ajar while the chicken rests.) Season the vegetables to taste with salt, if needed.

7. Carve the chicken, letting its juices run in the platter. Heap the chicken in the center of the platter. Using a slotted spoon, add the vegetables and herbs to the platter and serve.

BRAISED CHICKEN WITH WINE, OLIVES, AND GARLIC

Pollo al vino bianco

• •

Makes 4 servings

The best word to describe this dish is succulent. It's a classic example of country cooking showing that usually the best dishes have the fewest ingredients. The carrots add a spark of color and also some sweetness to balance the acidity of the wine. The trick with cooking a cut-up chicken is to give the dark meat (which takes longer to cook than the lean white meat) a head start in the skillet. Serve with bread to spread the softened garlic flesh.

1 chicken, cut into 8 serving pieces (about 3½ pounds)
Sea salt and freshly ground black pepper
2 tablespoons extra-virgin olive oil
16 garlic cloves, unpeeled, papery outer husk discarded

1½ cups dry white wine, such as Vernaccia
One 3-inch sprig of fresh thyme
3 medium carrots, preferably rainbow carrots, cut into ½-inch rounds
½ cup pitted and coarsely chopped dry-cured olives

1. Season the chicken with the salt and pepper. Heat the oil in a large deep skillet over medium-high heat. In batches, add the chicken, skin side down, and cook, until the skin is golden brown, about 3 minutes. Flip the chicken and brown the other side, about 3 minutes more. Transfer to a plate, leaving the fat in the pan.

2. Add the garlic cloves to the pan and cook, turning occasionally, until the skins are lightly browned, about 2 minutes. Add the wine and bring to a boil, scraping up the browned bits in the pan. Add the thyme. Return the drumsticks, thighs, and wings, with any juices, to the skillet. Cover tightly and reduce the heat to medium low. Cook, turning occasionally, for 15 minutes. Tuck the breast pieces among the chicken in the skillet. Continue cooking until the breast shows no sign of pink when pierced in the thickest part of the breast with a small sharp knife, about 25 minutes. Do not overcook. Transfer the chicken pieces to a deep platter, keeping the pan juices in the skillet. Tent the chicken with aluminum foil to keep it warm.

3. While the chicken is cooking, bring a small saucepan of salted water to a boil. Add the carrots and cook until they are barely tender, about 5 minutes. Drain the carrots, rinse them under cold running water, drain again, and set them aside.

4. Bring the cooking juices in the skillet to a boil over high heat. Cook until reduced by about half, 3 to 5 minutes. During the last minute, add the olives and reserved carrots. Discard the thyme sprig. Season to taste with the salt and pepper. Return the chicken to the skillet and turn to coat with the pan sauce. Return to the platter. Cut each breast in half crosswise, if desired. Serve immediately, with the garlic cloves. Let each guest smash the garlic with a fork to release the garlic flesh into the sauce and remove the garlic skin before eating.

CHICKEN SALTIMBOCCA

Saltimbocca di pollo

• •

Wine Pairing: Pinot Grigio or Vernaccia
Makes 4 servings

G: *In Italian cooking there are accepted formulas for specific recipes and, frankly, not too much experimentation. When you ask for saltimbocca, you will get veal cutlets topped with prosciutto with a sage leaf. But even a purist like myself will make an exception for this chicken-based version. My girls like chicken breast because it is lean, and I like to prepare it this way to be sure it has more flavor than usual. Be sure to pound the chicken to a uniform thickness (about ⅓ inch) so it cooks evenly (see Tip, page 197). One of the reasons boneless chicken breast is difficult to keep from drying out is because it is thick in the middle and thin at the ends.*

D: *I love everything about chicken breasts. They are easy to prep, cook quickly, and are very versatile. Serve this with the Golden Roasted Potatoes (page 216) and a green vegetable, and you are good to go.*

Special equipment: wooden toothpicks

4 skinless, boneless chicken breast halves (about 7 ounces each)
4 thin, wide slices prosciutto, cut in half crosswise to make 8 pieces
8 large sage leaves

Sea salt and freshly ground black pepper
¼ cup (35 grams) unbleached all-purpose flour
2 tablespoons unsalted butter
2 tablespoons extra-virgin olive oil
¾ cup dry white wine, such as Pinot Grigio

1. Cut each chicken breast half in two vertically to make 8 pieces total. One at a time, place a chicken portion between two plastic storage bags or sheets of plastic wrap. Using a flat meat mallet (or even a wine bottle or rolling pin), pound until about ⅓ inch thick throughout.

2. One at a time, place a chicken breast portion on the work surface. Top with a piece of prosciutto and a sage leaf. Using a wooden toothpick, attach the sage and prosciutto onto the chicken. Turn the chicken over and season the underside (not the prosciutto side) with the salt and pepper. (If you salt the side that touches the prosciutto, it could be too salty.) Spread the flour on a plate. Dredge the bare underside of the chicken in the flour and shake off the excess.

3. Position a rack in the center of the oven and preheat the oven to 200°F.

4. Heat the butter and the oil in a large skillet over medium-high heat until the butter is melted and the foam subsides. Add 4 of the chicken portions to the skillet, prosciutto side down. Cook until the prosciutto is browned, about 3 minutes. Turn the chicken over and cook until the other side

is browned and the chicken feels firm when pressed on top, about 3 minutes more. Transfer the chicken to a rimmed baking sheet and place in the oven. Repeat with the remaining chicken.

5. Pour out the fat in the skillet and return the skillet to medium-high heat. Add the wine to the skillet and bring to a boil, scraping up the browned bits in the skillet with a wooden spoon. Boil until the wine is reduced by half, about 3 minutes. Transfer the chicken to a platter. Remove the wooden toothpicks. Pour the pan sauce on top and serve immediately.

TIP It's a good idea to pound boneless and skinless chicken breast halves into uniform thickness so they cook more evenly. These days, with chicken breasts getting larger all the time, the breast halves are shaped like a humpbacked whale. This lumpy shape tends to result in overcooked ends and undercooked centers. Pounding the chicken to a thickness of about ⅓ inch throughout solves the problem.

CRISPY CHICKEN STRIPS WITH SPICY PESTO DIP

Filetti di pollo con salsa piccante

• •

Beer Pairing: Belgian-style pale ale
Serves 4

G: *Milan is famous for its breaded foods, with veal cutlets topping the list. We like to apply this treatment to chicken breasts and turn them into a finger food that we can all enjoy as our home-cooked version of chicken strips. When cooking the strips, be generous with the cooking oil. If it is too shallow, the coating will be soggy and not crispy. As for the dip, we are slightly addicted to sriracha, so even if it isn't very Italian, we use it here—but any hot sauce will do. By the way, in classic Italian cuisine,* alla milanese *means breaded and fried with lemon wedges, but we're serving it with the dip because the girls love it so much that way.*

SPICY PESTO DIP
1½ cups Mayonnaise (page 158)
3 tablespoons finely chopped fresh basil
2 tablespoons freshly grated Parmigiano-
  Reggiano cheese
1 garlic clove, crushed through a press or
  minced
1 teaspoon hot red sauce, such as sriracha, or
  ½ teaspoon hot red pepper flakes

1½ pounds skinless, boneless chicken breast
  halves
1 teaspoon sea salt
½ teaspoon freshly ground black pepper
½ cup (70 grams) unbleached all-purpose flour
3 large eggs
1 cup plain dried bread crumbs
Canola or vegetable oil, for frying

1. To make the dip: Mix the mayonnaise, basil, Parmigiano, garlic, and hot red sauce in a medium bowl.

2. One at a time, place a chicken portion between two plastic storage bags or sheets of plastic wrap. Using a flat meat mallet (or even a wine bottle or rolling pin), pound until about ⅓ inch thick throughout. Cut the chicken across the grain into ½-inch-wide strips. Season the chicken with the salt and pepper.

3. Spread the flour in a shallow bowl. Beat the eggs until combined in a second shallow bowl. Spread the bread crumbs in a third bowl. Line a platter with waxed or parchment paper.

4. Position a rack in the center of the oven and preheat the oven to 200°F. Set a wire cooling rack on a large rimmed baking sheet.

5. A few at a time, dredge the strips in flour, shaking off the excess. Dip in the eggs to coat, and roll in the crumbs to cover completely. Transfer to the lined platter.

6. Pour enough oil to come to about ¼ inch up the sides of large skillet. Do not skimp on the oil. Heat over medium-high heat until the oil is very hot and shimmering, but not smoking. In

batches without crowding, fry the chicken strips in the oil, turning them as needed, until golden brown, about 2½ minutes. Using a wire spider or slotted spoon, transfer the strips to the wire rack and keep warm in the oven while frying the remaining chicken. Just before serving, drain briefly on paper towels and transfer to a clean platter. Serve hot with the pesto dip.

TIP Draining fried foods on a wire rack is better than placing them on paper towels. The rack allows the air to circulate around the food. If the food sits directly on paper, steam forms on the underside, and that will soften the crust. If you wish, you can drain the food very briefly on paper towels or brown paper just before serving.

PANCETTA-WRAPPED TURKEY BREAST WITH HERBS

Tacchino in crosta di pancetta

· ·

Wine Pairing: Müller-Thurgau or Pinot Grigio
Makes 4 to 6 servings

We rarely serve the traditional Thanksgiving meal unless we have a full table of family expecting the tried-and-true dishes. Instead, we might serve this boneless turkey breast, rolled with herbs, wrapped in pancetta, and roasted to a turn. Each turkey slice looks beautiful with its swirl of herbs. We serve this with a white wine–based pan sauce, and the next day, leftovers make incredible sandwiches.

Special equipment: kitchen twine

1 skinless, boneless turkey breast half (about 1¾ pounds)
Sea salt and freshly ground black pepper
1 teaspoon finely chopped fresh rosemary
1 teaspoon finely chopped fresh sage

1 teaspoon finely chopped fresh thyme
16 slices pancetta (see Note, page 203)
1 tablespoon extra-virgin olive oil
½ cup dry white wine, such as Pinot Grigio

1. Position a rack in the center of the oven and preheat the oven to 350°F.

2. Place the turkey breast on a work surface, with the smaller pointed ends running vertically. Holding a thin sharp knife at a 45-degree angle, make a deep incision into the thickest part of the meat, making sure not to go all the way through the turkey meat. Open up this flap of meat like a book. Make a couple of other incisions in other thick areas of the turkey meat and open the flaps to widen the surface of the turkey to about 12 inches across. Season the turkey all over with the salt and pepper, placing the smoother side down. Sprinkle the turkey with the rosemary, sage, and thyme. Starting at a long side, roll up the turkey.

3. Shingle the pancetta slices on a piece of waxed or parchment paper so they form a 10-inch square. Place the rolled up turkey, seam side down, in the center of the pancetta square. Using the waxed paper as an aid, bring up the paper with the pancetta to wrap the turkey. Using kitchen twine, tie the pancetta onto the turkey.

4. Heat the oil in a large ovenproof skillet over medium heat. Add the turkey roll and cook, turning occasionally, until the pancetta is translucent and partially cooked all over, but not browned, about 5 minutes.

5. Transfer the skillet with the turkey to the oven. Bake, turning occasionally, until an instant-read thermometer inserted into the center of the roll reads 160°F and the pancetta is browned, about 50 minutes. Remove from the oven. Transfer the roll to a platter and let stand for about 5 minutes.

6. Meanwhile, pour any fat out of the skillet. Heat the skillet over medium-high heat until the juices are sizzling. Add the wine and bring to a boil, scraping up the browned bits in the skillet with a wooden spoon. Cook until reduced by half, about 3 minutes. Remove the skillet from the heat.

7. Cut and remove the kitchen twine. Using a thin sharp knife, cut the roll crosswise into ½-inch slices, and fan the slices on the platter. Pour the skillet sauce all over the turkey and serve.

NOTE The pancetta should be sliced about as thick as American bacon, not paper-thin like prosciutto.

VEGETABLES AND GRAINS

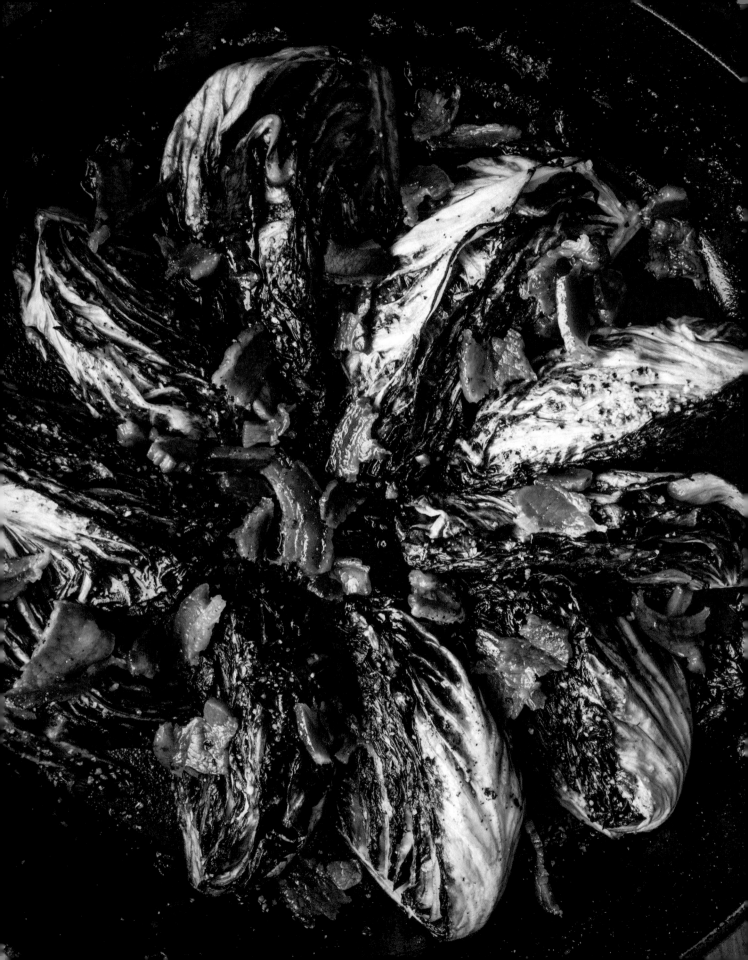

ROASTED RADICCHIO AND PANCETTA

Radicchio e pancetta al forno

• •

Makes 4 to 6 servings

G: *Radicchio is considered a salad vegetable in America, but we Italians appreciate its versatility as a cooking vegetable too. With only a few ingredients, and a little seasoning, this is a super-simple dish that you can toss together in no time. Roasting deepens the radicchio's flavor and adds a touch of sweetness too. Try this alongside a sautéed halibut or cod fillet, or with your favorite roast chicken.*

1 tablespoon extra-virgin olive oil, plus more for serving
2 slices pancetta

2 heads radicchio, root ends trimmed (about 6 ounces each)
Sea salt and freshly ground black pepper

1. Position a rack in the center of the oven and preheat the oven to 400°F.

2. Heat the oil in a large ovenproof skillet over medium heat. Add the pancetta and cook, turning once, until crisp and browned, 3 to 5 minutes. Transfer the pancetta to a paper-towel-lined plate to drain, leaving the fat in the skillet.

3. Quarter each radicchio lengthwise. Place the radicchio, cut side down, in the skillet and cook until the underside is lightly browned, about 2 minutes. Turn to lightly brown the other cut side, about 2 minutes more. Season to taste with the salt and pepper.

4. Transfer the skillet with the radicchio to the oven and bake until the radicchio is tender, about 10 minutes. Transfer the radicchio to a serving dish. Crumble the pancetta on top, drizzle with olive oil, and serve.

PAN-ROASTED GREEN BEANS

Fagiolini saltati col guanciale

....

Makes 4 servings

Very often you need a bright green vegetable, simply prepared, to round out a menu and add a splash of color. That's where this side dish comes in. Green beans and bacon are a familiar American combination, but guanciale gives this a distinctly Tuscan feel. The trick is to cook these just long enough, and to make sure that they don't turn olive green and mushy.

1 tablespoon extra-virgin olive oil
¼ cup (¼-inch) diced guanciale or pancetta
2 tablespoons finely chopped shallots

1 pound green beans, cut into 2-inch lengths or
  left whole
½ cup dry white wine or water
Sea salt and freshly ground black pepper

1. Heat the oil in a large skillet over medium heat. Add the guanciale and cook, stirring occasionally, until browned, about 3 minutes. Add the shallots and cook, stirring often, until softened, about 1 minute.

2. Add the green beans and stir well. Add the wine, cover tightly, and cook, stirring occasionally, until the green beans are crisp-tender and the liquid evaporates, about 5 minutes. Season to taste with the salt and pepper and serve.

TREVISO RADICCHIO WITH CANNELLINI BEANS

Radicchio di Treviso e fagioli cannellini

• •

Makes 6 servings

This versatile mix of tender white beans and earthy radicchio would be great with roast lamb or pork (especially our Roasted Spareribs with Tomato-Wine Sauce, page 179), or use it as a bed for grilled or sautéed chops. We prefer the elongated Treviso radicchio in this dish for its tailored appearance, but the familiar round variety works well too.

¼ cup extra-virgin olive oil, plus more for drizzling
1 medium yellow onion, finely chopped
2 anchovy fillets in oil, drained and finely chopped
3 garlic cloves, finely chopped

1 teaspoon finely chopped fresh rosemary
Two 15-ounce cans cannellini (white kidney) beans, drained
Sea salt and freshly ground black pepper
1 head Treviso radicchio or ½ large head round radicchio, cored and cut into thin strips

1. Heat the oil in a large skillet over medium heat. Add the onion and cook until tender, about 4 minutes. Stir in the anchovies, garlic, and rosemary. Stir constantly until the anchovies melt into the onions and the garlic is fragrant, about 1 minute. Add the beans and ½ cup water. Bring to a simmer and reduce the heat to medium low. Cook until the beans are heated through, about 5 minutes. Using a wooden spoon, mash some of the beans to thicken the liquid and give it a creamy consistency. Season to taste with the salt and pepper.

2. Put the radicchio in a serving bowl. Add the hot beans and stir well—the heat of the beans will wilt the radicchio. Season to taste with the salt and pepper. Drizzle with oil and serve immediately.

CHAINED POLENTA WITH PARMIGIANO AND KALE

Polenta incatenata

• •

Makes 4 to 6 servings

Most of the time, when we make smooth and comforting polenta, it is simply cooked with water and served as a side dish with a flavorful sauced main course, such as a pot roast or stew. But traditionally, in the Tuscan mountainsides during the winter months when food is scarce, this kind of polenta is made as a way to stretch kale, one of the few things that grows during that time of year. It is called polenta incatenata *("chained" polenta) because the polenta latches on to the other ingredients to make it more nourishing. When we first had Southern collards and grits, it reminded us of this dish.*

2 bunches black (also called lacinato, Tuscan, or dinosaur) kale, tough stems removed (about 14 ounces total)
2 cups Vegetable Broth (page 67), Chicken Stock (page 55), or more water

2 cups whole milk
½ teaspoon sea salt
2 cups instant polenta
½ cup freshly grated Parmigiano-Reggiano cheese

1. Bring a medium saucepan of salted water to a boil over high heat. Stir in the kale and cook for 2 minutes. Drain, rinse under cold running water, and drain again. Let cool until easy to handle. Squeeze out the excess moisture and coarsely chop the kale.

2. Bring 2 cups water, the broth, milk, and salt to a boil in a large saucepan over medium heat. Whisk in the polenta and cook until it comes to a boil. Reduce the heat to low and cook, whisking often, until the polenta is tender, about 3 minutes. Remove from the heat. Stir in the kale and Parmigiano. Transfer to a bowl and serve immediately.

STUFFED ZUCCHINI WITH RICOTTA AND HERBS

Zucchini ripieni con erbe e ricotta

● ●

Makes 4 servings

When we think of stuffed vegetables, it bring us back to summertime in Tuscany, where the garden produces so much (is that why it is called produce?) that we never find enough uses for it. Prolific zucchini is one of the prime offenders. Here it is, stuffed with ricotta and Parmigiano for a dish that can be served with meat and poultry, or enjoyed as a vegetarian main course. Either way, we feel it is more versatile served without tomato sauce, but add some if you wish.

1 tablespoon extra-virgin olive oil, plus more for
   oiling and drizzling
4 medium zucchini (about 6 ounces each)
½ teaspoon sea salt, plus more for seasoning
1 medium yellow onion, finely chopped
1 garlic clove, minced
1 cup ricotta cheese

⅓ cup freshly grated Parmigiano-Reggiano
   cheese
3 tablespoons plain dried bread crumbs
Freshly ground black pepper
1 tablespoon finely chopped fresh basil or flat-
   leaf parsley, for serving

1. Position a rack in the upper third of the oven and preheat to 350°F. Lightly oil a 9 by 13-inch baking dish.

2. Cut each zucchini in half lengthwise. Using a dessertspoon, scrape out the flesh to make shells about ½ inch thick. Coarsely chop the flesh and set it aside. Sprinkle the insides of the zucchini halves with the salt. Set aside in a colander to extrude excess liquid for 30 minutes to 1 hour. Rinse the zucchini and pat them dry.

3. Heat the oil in a medium skillet over medium heat. Add the zucchini flesh and cook, stirring occasionally, until lightly browned, about 3 minutes. Move the zucchini to one side of the pan. Add the onion and garlic to the opposite side and cook, occasionally stirring the onion mixture only, until the onion is softened, about 3 minutes. Mix together and transfer to a medium bowl. Add the ricotta, Parmigiano, and 2 tablespoons of the bread crumbs. Season to taste with the salt and pepper.

4. Place the zucchini shells in the dish and fill with the ricotta mixture. Sprinkle with the remaining 1 tablespoon bread crumbs and drizzle with the oil. Cover tightly with aluminum foil.

5. Bake for 20 minutes. Uncover and bake until the zucchini is tender when pierced in the side with the tip of a small sharp knife, about 15 minutes more. Sprinkle with the basil and serve.

STUFFED ONIONS WITH ARUGULA

Cipolle ripiene alla rucola

••

Makes 8 servings

D: *During harvest season in Italy, the local farms are bursting with produce, and everyone becomes a bit of a vegetarian for a while. Gabriele's grandmother, Nonna Lola, is the Queen of the Vegetable Stuffers, and can take the most humble vegetables and turn them into something mouthwatering. This recipe—plump red onions parboiled and filled with peppery green arugula—pays homage to her, and it is fantastic next to a grilled steak or pork chops. In Lola's kosher kitchen, however, a few minced anchovies substitute for the guanciale, and you can do the same.*

1 tablespoon plus 4 teaspoons extra-virgin olive oil, plus more for oiling and serving

4 medium red onions, unpeeled (about 7 ounces each)

½ cup boiling water

⅓ cup (¼-inch) diced guanciale or pancetta

1 garlic clove, chopped

1 cup coarsely chopped and packed arugula

½ cup plain dried bread crumbs

4 tablespoons freshly grated Pecorino Romano cheese

Sea salt and freshly ground black pepper

2 tablespoons finely chopped fresh flat-leaf parsley, for serving

1. Position a rack in the center of the oven and preheat the oven to 350°F. Lightly oil a 9 by 13-inch baking dish.

2. Cut each onion in half from the top to the root end (not through its equator). Using a dessertspoon, scoop out the center of each onion to make a cup about ½ inch thick, reserving the onion trimmings. Arrange the onion cups, skin side down, in the prepared dish. Drizzle with 2 teaspoons of the olive oil and pour the boiling water around the cups. Cover tightly with aluminum foil. Bake until the cups are softened but hold their shape, about 20 minutes.

3. Meanwhile, finely chop the onion trimmings. Cook the guanciale, chopped onion, and 1 tablespoon of the olive oil in a medium skillet over medium heat, stirring occasionally, until the onion is tender and the guanciale is browned, about 5 minutes. Stir in the garlic and cook just until fragrant. Transfer to a medium bowl and stir in the arugula, bread crumbs, and 2 tablespoons of the Pecorino. Season to taste with the salt and pepper.

4. Remove the dish with the onion cups from the oven. Uncover and fill the cups with the chopped onion mixture. Sprinkle with the remaining 2 tablespoons Pecorino and drizzle with the remaining 2 teaspoons oil. Return to the oven and bake, uncovered, until the tops are golden brown and the onions are tender, about 20 minutes. Transfer to a serving platter. Sprinkle with the parsley, drizzle with the oil, and serve.

GOLDEN ROASTED POTATOES

Patate arrosto

••••••••••••••••••••••••••••••••••••

Makes 6 to 8 servings

It was our Australian friend, Simon Andrews, this book's food stylist, who turned us on to these very special potatoes. Golden and crusty on the outside, and tender within, these are a variation on traditional plain roasted potatoes. The potatoes are parboiled and then dried out in the cooking pot to give them a scuffed surface, and this roughing-up gives the exteriors an amazingly tasty crust. We love these with big meat roasts, such as the Roast Leg of Lamb with Garlic and Rosemary or Roast Beef with Baby Onions (pages 183 and 163).

3 pounds baking potatoes, peeled, cut in halves lengthwise and then into 2-inch chunks

½ cup extra-virgin olive oil, plus more as needed

2 teaspoons finely chopped fresh thyme or rosemary (optional)

Flaky sea salt, such as Maldon or fleur de sel, and freshly ground black pepper

1. Place the potatoes and add enough cold salted water to cover the potatoes by 1 inch. Cover and bring to a boil over high heat. Uncover and reduce the heat to medium. Cook at a steady simmer until the potatoes soften on the outside, about 5 minutes. Drain well.

2. Return the empty cooking pot to low heat. Add the drained potatoes and cook, occasionally turning them over in the pot, until the surfaces look rough and somewhat drier, 1 to 2 minutes. Remove the pot from the heat.

3. Meanwhile, position a rack in the center of the oven and preheat the oven to 350°F. Pour enough oil (about ½ cup) into a large roasting pan to come about ¹⁄₁₆ inch up the sides. Heat the pan with the oil in the oven until the oil is very hot, but not smoking, 3 to 5 minutes. Remove the pan from the oven. In a single layer, carefully arrange the potatoes, flat sides down, in the hot oil. (Remember, the oil is hot, so don't splash it.)

4. Place the pan back in the oven and roast until the undersides are golden and can be easily turned with a metal spatula without sticking, about 30 minutes. Turn the potatoes over and continue roasting until crisp and golden, about 30 minutes more. Using a slotted spoon, transfer the potatoes to a serving dish. Sprinkle with the thyme, if using, and season to taste with the salt and pepper. Serve hot.

POTATO CROQUETTES

Crocchette di patate

••••••••••••••••••••••••••

Makes 16 croquettes

G: *My mom was a very busy schoolteacher, and on Saturdays, she worked half a day in the morning. She would finish her job, pick my brother, Fabio, and me up from our school, drive to the local* rosticceria, *and buy roast chicken and potato croquettes for lunch. On the way home, the aroma of the chicken and potatoes would drive us crazy, and we would tear into them when we got to the table. Croquettes are basically fried mashed potatoes, but* what *mashed potatoes! If you can, serve the croquettes hot out of the oil; however, they can also be cooled and warmed up in a 350°F oven for about 10 minutes. After all, that's what Mom did.*

2 pounds baking potatoes, such as russets, peeled

1 cup freshly grated Parmigiano-Reggiano cheese

2 large eggs, beaten to blend

1½ teaspoons sea salt

¼ teaspoon freshly ground black pepper

A few gratings of whole nutmeg

½ cup (70 grams) unbleached all-purpose flour, plus more for rolling

3 large eggs

1 cup plain dried bread crumbs

Vegetable oil, for deep-frying

Finely chopped fresh parsley, for serving

1. Place the potatoes in a large pot, add cold salted water to cover by 1 inch, and cover. Bring to a boil over high heat. Reduce the heat to medium low. Simmer until the potatoes are tender when pierced with the tip of a sharp knife, 20 to 25 minutes, depending on their size. Drain and rinse under cold running water to stop the cooking. Let the potatoes cool completely, uncovered, for at least 2 hours, or overnight. It's fine if the surface dries out. You want the potatoes as dry as possible.

2. Run the potatoes through a potato ricer (see Tip, page 136) or a food mill fitted with the coarse blade into a large bowl. (Or rub the potatoes through a coarse mesh sieve with a wooden spoon.) Mix in the Parmigiano, eggs, salt, pepper, and nutmeg.

3. Spread the flour in a shallow bowl. Beat the eggs well in a second bowl. Spread the bread crumbs in a third bowl. Generously dust a baking sheet with flour and place it near the work area. Line a platter with parchment or waxed paper.

4. Coat your hands with flour. One at a time, shape about 3 tablespoons of the potato mixture into fat finger shapes, about 3 inches long with rounded ends, and transfer to the baking sheet. Roll the cylinder in the flour to help shape it into a neat log. Dip each in the eggs to coat, roll in the bread crumbs to coat, and place on the parchment-paper-lined platter. Repeat until all of the mixture has been used. Let the croquettes stand while heating the oil.

5. Line a second baking sheet with paper towels and place it near the stove. Pour enough oil to come halfway up the sides of a large saucepan and heat over high heat until the oil reaches 350°F on a deep-frying thermometer. In batches without crowding, use a wire spider or slotted spoon to carefully add the croquettes to the oil. Deep-fry until they are golden brown, about 3 minutes. Using the spider, transfer the croquettes to the paper towel-lined baking sheet to drain briefly. Discard the parchment paper on the platter, and move the croquettes to the platter. Sprinkle with the parsley and serve warm.

LOLA'S POTATO GRATIN

Patate gratinate

• •

Makes 6 servings

There is one thing about potato gratin: It can't be rushed. Set aside some time to make it and savor the creamy results. Aka scalloped potatoes or potatoes au gratin, this golden masterpiece is an essential recipe that every cook should know how to make. Here is our version, which uses earthy fontina cheese and a bit of sharp Parmigiano. We sometimes swap out the cheeses according to the bits and pieces of leftover cheese that need to be used up—they are all different; they are all worth eating!

Softened unsalted butter, for the baking dish, and aluminum foil
1 cup whole milk
1 cup heavy cream
½ teaspoon sea salt
¼ teaspoon freshly ground black pepper

2 pounds baking potatoes, such as russets, peeled and cut into ¹⁄₁₆-inch rounds
1 cup (4 ounces) shredded fontina cheese, preferably Fontina Val d'Aosta
2 tablespoons freshly grated Parmigiano-Reggiano cheese

1. Position a rack in the center of the oven and preheat the oven to 350°F. Butter an 11 by 8½-inch baking dish.

2. Bring the milk and cream to a simmer in a medium saucepan over medium heat. Reduce the heat to the lowest setting.

3. Mix the salt and pepper together. Spread one-third of the potatoes in the prepared dish and season with one-third of the salt mixture. Top with one-half of the fontina. Repeat and finish with a layer of potatoes. Pour the hot milk mixture evenly over the potatoes. Press on the potatoes to be sure that they are submerged in the liquid. Sprinkle with the Parmigiano.

4. Place the dish on a baking sheet. Cover the dish with buttered aluminum foil, buttered side down. Bake for 45 minutes. Remove the foil and continue baking until the potatoes are tender when pierced with the tip of a small knife and the gratin is golden brown, about 45 minutes more. Let stand for 5 minutes and serve hot.

MASHED POTATOES WITH MASCARPONE

Purè di patate al mascarpone

●●

Makes 6 to 8 servings

Most of us are used to making mashed potatoes in the time-honored way with butter and cream. That's the way both of our grandmothers made them, and we have no argument. But mascarpone is both buttery and creamy, and it is a great alternative to the old method. The cheese gives the potatoes a slight tang too. For a special occasion, take them a step higher with some chives. Be sure the mascarpone is at room temperature, as you want to do everything possible to keep the potatoes hot. These are the perfect mashed potatoes all'italiana.

3 pounds baking potatoes, such as russets, peeled and cut into 1-inch chunks
½ cup mascarpone cheese, at room temperature

Sea salt and freshly ground black pepper
3 tablespoons finely chopped fresh chives (optional)

1. Bring a large saucepan of salted water to a boil over high heat. Add the potatoes, cover the saucepan, and return the water to a boil. Reduce the heat to medium low to keep the water at a steady low boil. Set the lid ajar and cook until the potatoes can be pierced with the tip of a sharp knife, 15 to 20 minutes.

2. Place a heatproof serving bowl in the sink. Drain the potatoes, letting the hot water fill and warm the bowl. Return the drained potatoes to the saucepan. Cook over low heat, stirring almost constantly, until the potatoes begin to film the bottom of the saucepan, about 2 minutes. Remove from the heat.

3. Using a handheld potato masher or an electric hand mixer, mash (or beat) the potatoes until they are broken up. (Or transfer the potatoes to a bowl and push them through a potato ricer back into the saucepan.) Continue mashing (or beating), gradually adding the mascarpone. (If using a ricer, gradually stir it in with a wooden spoon.) Season to taste with the salt and pepper. Stir in the chives, if using. Drain the water from the bowl, dry it quickly, add the mashed potatoes, and serve.

COUSCOUS WITH CHERRY TOMATOES AND OLIVES

Cuscus Mediterraneo

••

Makes 4 to 6 servings

Couscous is ready in just a few minutes, and its only drawback is that it can be a bit bland. To fix this, we prepare it with a quick sauté of cherry tomatoes and olives to give it a Mediterranean-flavored boost. This is a great side dish for the Marinated Lamb Sauté with Cucumber-Yogurt Sauce (page 181).

2 tablespoons extra-virgin olive oil
½ teaspoon sea salt, plus more for seasoning
1 cup couscous
1 cup quartered cherry tomatoes
¼ teaspoon hot red pepper flakes

⅓ cup pitted and coarsely chopped black Mediterranean olives
2 tablespoons chopped fresh cilantro
Freshly ground black pepper

1. Bring 1 cup water, 1 tablespoon of the oil, and ½ teaspoon of the salt to a boil in a medium sauce-pan over high heat. Stir in the couscous, remove from the heat, and cover tightly. Let stand until the couscous is tender and has absorbed the liquid, 5 to 10 minutes.

2. Meanwhile, heat the remaining 1 tablespoon oil in a large nonstick skillet over medium-high heat. Add the cherry tomatoes and red pepper flakes and cook until the tomatoes are warm, about 2 minutes. Stir in the olives and cook, stirring occasionally, until the tomatoes begin to col-lapse, about 2 minutes more. Fluffing the couscous with a fork, add to the skillet. Add the cilantro and mix well. Season to taste with the salt and black pepper. Serve hot.

FARRO WITH MUSHROOMS AND BABY SPINACH

Farro con funghi e spinaci

•••

Makes 4 to 6 servings

G: *Everyone knows about the importance of grains in your diet. I'd much rather eat farro than brown rice any day. While there is nothing wrong with plain farro, here is an easy way to dress it up. Mushrooms play up the grain's rustic flavor and spinach adds color to make a side dish that has both starch and vegetables.*

1 cup semi-pearled farro
2 tablespoons extra-virgin olive oil
10 ounces cremini mushrooms, sliced
2 tablespoons finely chopped shallots
1 garlic clove, minced
1 teaspoon finely chopped fresh thyme

2 packed cups baby spinach leaves (about
  2 ounces)
¼ cup freshly grated Parmigiano-Reggiano
  cheese
Sea salt and freshly ground black pepper

1. Bring a medium saucepan of lightly salted water to a boil over high heat. Add the farro and reduce the heat to medium. Cook at a steady boil until the farro is tender, about 20 minutes. (If you have whole grain farro, cook about 45 minutes.) Drain well.

2. Meanwhile, heat the oil in a large skillet over medium-high heat. Add the mushrooms and cook, stirring occasionally, until they begin to brown, about 6 minutes. Stir in the shallots and garlic and reduce the heat to low. Cook, stirring often, until they soften, about 1 minute. (The pan is hot so this won't take long.) Stir in the thyme.

3. Reduce the heat to low. Stir in the hot farro. In batches, stir in the spinach and cook just until wilted, about 2 minutes. Remove from the heat and stir in the Parmigiano. Season to taste with the salt and pepper. Serve hot.

SWISS CHARD WITH GARBANZO BEANS

Bietole e ceci

• •

Makes 4 to 6 servings

We like to put Swiss chard on the table as the meal's vegetable because, like other leafy greens, it has lots of nutritional benefits. However, it can be a little bland, so add a few other ingredients like pancetta, shallot, and garbanzo beans to give it a lift. As the beans cook, they break down a little to thicken the cooking juices. We also like this heaped onto bruschetta as an antipasto or light lunch.

2 pounds Swiss chard, preferably rainbow chard
2 tablespoons extra-virgin olive oil
2 ounces pancetta, cut into ¼-inch dice (about ½ cup)

2 tablespoons finely chopped shallot
Pinch of hot red pepper flakes
One 15-ounce can garbanzo beans (chickpeas), drained and rinsed
Sea salt and freshly ground black pepper

1. Wash the chard leaves and stems well in a large sink of cold water. Lift the chard out of the water, leaving the grit at the bottom of the sink. Shake off the excess water, but do not dry the chard.

2. Tear the stems from the leaves and chop the stems crosswise into ½-inch pieces. Stack the leaves and coarsely chop them. Keep the stems and leaves separate.

3. Heat the oil in a large skillet over medium-high heat. Add the pancetta and cook until it is crisp and browned, about 3 minutes. Stir in the shallot and red pepper flakes and cook, stirring often, until the shallot softens, about 2 minutes.

4. Add the chard stems and beans. Cook, stirring occasionally, until the stems soften, about 4 minutes. A handful at a time, stir in the leaves. Cover and cook, stirring occasionally, until the chard is tender, about 5 minutes. Season to taste with the salt and pepper. Serve hot.

DESSERTS

ITALIAN CARROT CAKE

Torta di carote

• •

Makes 8 to 10 servings

G: *To an American, carrot cake means a rich spiced cake frosted with super-sweet cream cheese icing. But to a Tuscan, this moist cake has no spices at all. In fact, cinnamon is rarely used in desserts and only occasionally used in some savory cooking, such as Barolo Pot Roast on page 165. This recipe comes straight from my family recipe box. Served with the mascarpone cream, it is a lovely dinner party dessert, but it also works well with your morning espresso or afternoon coffee. Try to let the cake stand overnight before serving so the flavors settle.*

CARROT CAKE
Softened unsalted butter, for the pan
⅔ cup (95 grams) unbleached all-purpose flour
One 16-gram package Italian baking powder
    (see page 230) or 2½ teaspoons American
    baking powder
2 cups (200 grams) blanched almond flour
5 large eggs, separated, at room temperature
1¼ cups granulated sugar
3 cups shredded carrots, from about 4 medium
    carrots (11 ounces after shredding)
¼ teaspoon sea salt
1 teaspoon vanilla (if using American baking
    powder)

MASCARPONE CREAM
1 cup mascarpone cheese
2 tablespoons confectioners' sugar

Confectioners' sugar, for sifting
1 orange, for zesting (optional)

1. Position a rack in the center of the oven and preheat the oven to 350°F. Lightly butter a 9-inch springform pan.

2. To make the carrot cake: Whisk the flour and baking powder into a large bowl. Add the almond flour and whisk again. Beat the egg yolks and granulated sugar in a separate large bowl with an electric hand mixer set at high speed, scraping down the sides as needed, until the mixture is thickened and pale yellow, about 2 minutes. (A hand mixer or a whisk works best. In a standing mixer, the yolks may not have enough volume for the whisk attachment to reach them in the bottom of a standing mixer's bowl.) Using a sturdy wooden spoon, gradually stir in the almond flour mixture, followed by the shredded carrots. If using the vanilla extract, stir in now. The batter will be quite thick at this point.

3. Using clean beaters, whip the egg whites with the salt in a medium grease-free bowl with the hand mixer set on high speed until they form stiff, but not dry, peaks. Using a rubber spatula, stir

about one-fourth of the whites into the carrot mixture to lighten it. Fold in the remaining whites. Spread the batter evenly in the prepared pan.

4. Bake until the cake is golden brown and has shrunk slightly from the pan, about 1 hour. Let the cake cool on a wire rack for 30 minutes. Remove the sides of the pan and let cool completely. (The cake can be wrapped in plastic wrap and stored at room temperature for up to 2 days. If possible, let the cake stand for at least 12 hours before serving.)

5. To make the mascarpone cream: Work the mascarpone and confectioners' sugar together in a small bowl until combined. Let stand at room temperature for about 1 hour to remove its chill.

6. Just before serving, sift confectioners' sugar over the cake. Slice and serve with a dollop of the mascarpone cream, topped with a grating of orange zest, if desired.

ITALIAN BAKING POWDER

Italian baking powder (*lievito*) is sold in boxes with 10 individual 16-gram envelopes, each holding about 4 teaspoons of leavening. One popular brand, Paneangeli, is easily found online and at Italian-American markets. Many Italian cake recipes call for "1 envelope baking powder" instead of measuring it out by the teaspoon. Do not confuse it with yeast for baking bread. This is especially confusing because Paneangeli also has the slogan "Lievito Pane degli Angeli," or "yeast bread of the angels," when it has nothing to do with bread! If you look closely on the label, it also says *per dolci* (for sweets) in tiny letters.

The active ingredients in Italian baking powder are somewhat different from those in the American variety, and the final baked goods vary accordingly. Some people find the crumb in cakes to be finer with the Italian leavening.

You will see the advice that the two baking powders are interchangeable, but that's not really so. (In other words, if an American recipe calls for 2 teaspoons baking powder, you *should* be able to substitute 2 teaspoons *lievito*. Actually there is the rising power of about 2½ teaspoons American baking powder and the flavor of about 1 teaspoon vanilla extract in each envelope of *lievito*. Rather than deal with substitutes, we recommend giving Italian baking powder a try. You'll find lots of recipes online (in Italian) that use it, and most browsers can now translate the pages for you.

FREE-FORM FIG CROSTATA WITH MASCARPONE

Crostata rustica di fichi con crema di mascarpone

• •

Makes 8 servings

While a molded crostata, or tart, is beautiful, here is an equally delicious free-form version that has a rustic appeal. This kind of crostata should be made with relatively firm fruit that won't give off a lot of juice, so figs are perfect. They will soften, but not break down into a filling like a fig cookie. Figs vary in sweetness, and Black Mission figs are one of the sweeter varieties. Feel free to substitute other kinds, such as the green Kadota or Sierra varieties, or Brown Turkey, and increase the sugar to 3 tablespoons.

CROSTATA DOUGH
1¼ cups (175 grams) unbleached all-purpose flour, plus more for rolling
3 tablespoons sugar
⅛ teaspoon sea salt
Finely grated zest of ½ lemon
4 ounces (1 stick) cold unsalted butter, cut into ½-inch cubes
2 tablespoons silver or golden rum, or grappa, as needed
1 large egg yolk
½ teaspoon vanilla extract or the seeds of ½ vanilla bean
Flour, for rolling the dough

1 pound Black Mission figs, stemmed and cut into quarters or halves, depending on their size
2 tablespoons granulated sugar
2 teaspoons fresh lemon juice
1 tablespoon heavy cream, plus more as needed
Demerara or turbinado sugar, for the crust (optional)
⅔ cup mascarpone cheese
2 tablespoons honey
2 teaspoons finely chopped fresh rosemary or thyme, for serving (optional)

1. To make the dough: Stir the flour, sugar, salt, and zest in a medium bowl. Add the butter. Using a pastry blender or two knives, cut the butter into the mixture until it resembles coarse crumbs with some pea-sized pieces of butter. (To make in a stand mixer: Combine the dry ingredients in the mixer bowl. Attach to the mixer and fit with the paddle attachment. Add the butter and mix on medium speed until the mixture resembles coarse crumbs, about 2 minutes. Do not over-mix.)

2. Whisk the rum, yolk, and vanilla in a small bowl. Drizzle over the flour mixture and stir (or mix on low speed) until moistened. The mixture may look dry, but should hold together when a handful is pressed in your fist. If necessary, sprinkle in more rum, a teaspoon at a time to get the correct consistency. Gather up the dough and shape into a thick disk. Wrap in plastic wrap and refrigerate until chilled but not hard, 45 minutes to 1 hour.

3. Position a rack in the bottom third of the oven and preheat the oven to 400°F. Flip a half-sheet pan over and line the underside of it with parchment paper or a silicone baking mat. (It is easier

to slide the baked crostata off a rimless surface, and an upturned half-sheet pan works perfectly. Most rimless baking sheets are not large enough to comfortably hold the crostata.)

4. Place the unwrapped dough on a well-floured surface, and dust the top of the dough with flour too. (If you wish, draw a 12-inch-diameter circle in the flour as a template to get the correct size for the dough.) Roll out the dough into a 12-inch round about $\frac{1}{8}$ inch thick, turning the dough over occasionally and slipping a long metal spatula underneath the round to be sure it isn't sticking. Transfer the dough to the prepared sheet pan or mat.

5. Mix the figs, granulated sugar, and lemon juice in a medium bowl. Spread the figs on the dough round, leaving a 2-inch border around the edges. Bring up the dough, gently pleating it as needed, to partially cover the fig filling. Brush the exposed crust lightly with some of the cream, and sprinkle with the Demerara sugar, if using. Bake until the crust is golden brown and the juices are thickened and bubbling, about 35 minutes.

6. Meanwhile, make the mascarpone: Mix the mascarpone and honey together in a small bowl. Cover and refrigerate until serving.

7. Let the crostata cool on the pan for 5 minutes. Slide it off the pan onto a serving platter. Cool for 10 minutes more, until warm, or let cool completely. Slice and serve with a dollop of the mascarpone and a sprinkle of rosemary, or just serve as is.

CROSTATA DOUGH TUTORIAL

Knowing how to roll out crostata dough (and, if needed, line a tart pan) is an essential technique in the Tuscan kitchen. We use it for three dessert crostini in this chapter: Free-Form Fig Crostata with Mascarpone, Double Peach Tart, and Chocolate and Raspberry Tart on pages 231, 235, and 237, as well as the savory Asparagus and Prosciutto Tortino on page 93.

1. Roll out the dough into a 12-inch round; mark the circle in the flour first to serve as a useful template.

2. Fit the dough into the pan, being sure that it fits snugly into the corners without stretching the dough.

3. Trim the excess dough by rolling the pin over the pan top, or press it away with the heel of your hand.

DOUBLE PEACH TART

Crostata alla confettura di pesche

•••••••••••••••••••••••••••

Makes 8 servings

D: *Peach pie made with our upstate New York peaches is my absolute favorite dessert. There is some-thing about its aroma filling the kitchen that just drives me crazy. I can hardly wait for it to cool down before I cut into it. When we visit Italy,* crostata alla confettura *is one of those beloved desserts that every mamma seems to have a recipe for, and the peach version is especially tasty. So this combines two beloved sweets into one super-dessert. The dough is very forgiving, so don't worry if it falls apart when you put it in the pan. And you may as well get some vanilla gelato to serve with this too.*

1 recipe Crostata Dough (page 231)
3 large ripe peaches, pitted and cut into ½-inch wedges
2 tablespoons sugar
1 tablespoon unbleached all-purpose flour
1 tablespoon unsalted butter, melted
¾ cup peach jam or preserves

1. Position a rack in the lower third of the oven and preheat the oven to 375°F.

2. Meanwhile, lightly dust the work surface with flour. Unwrap the dough and dust the top with flour too. Roll out the dough into a round about 12 inches in diameter and ⅛ inch thick. Trans-fer the dough to a tart pan, fitting the dough snugly into the corners without stretching it. If the dough breaks, just press it together. (Cursing is optional, but recommended.) Remove the excess dough around the top edge of the pan. Freeze the dough-lined pan for about 15 minutes.

3. Cover the dough with a sheet of aluminum foil and fill with pie weights or dried beans. Place on a baking sheet and bake until the exposed dough looks dry, about 10 minutes. Remove the pan from the oven. Lift up and remove the foil with the weights. Return to the oven and continue baking until the crust is just beginning to brown, about 10 minutes. Remove from the oven.

4. Toss the peaches, sugar, flour, and melted butter in a medium bowl, taking care not to break up the peaches. Spread half of the jam in the pastry shell. Arrange and overlap the peaches in a circle in the pastry shell, saving the smaller peaches to fill the empty space in the center of the circle. Scrape any liquid in the bowl over the peaches. Return to the oven until the pastry is golden brown, the jam is bubbling, and the peaches are tender, 30 to 40 minutes. Remove from the oven. Spoon the remaining jam over the peaches, using the back of the spoon to spread the jam and fill any gaps.

5. Let the tart cool on a wire rack for 15 minutes. Remove the sides of the pan and let cool com-pletely. Cut into slices and serve.

CHOCOLATE AND RASPBERRY TART

Crostata di cioccolato e lamponi

• •

Makes 8 servings

Once you learn how to make a crostata, you will have a large range of desserts at your fingertips. While the Double Peach Tart (page 235) has the filling baked in, here the crust is first fully baked and cooled, then filled with a luscious chocolate cream and topped with fruit. If you wish to glaze the fruit for a professional finish, melt ½ cup red currant jelly over low heat and use it to paint the raspberries. But we are very unfussy bakers, and the confectioners' sugar is our preferred topping.

1 recipe Crostata Dough (page 231)
¾ cup heavy cream
6 ounces semisweet chocolate (about 55% cacao), finely chopped

1 tablespoon grappa, brandy, or Cognac
3 cups fresh raspberries, as needed (about three 6-ounce containers)
Confectioners' sugar, for garnish

1. Make the crostata shell according to the directions on page 235, through step 3, but after removing the foil and weights, return the pan to the oven and continue baking until the shell is completely golden brown. Let the crostata shell cool in the pan on a wire cake rack.

2. Bring the cream to a simmer in a small saucepan over medium heat. Remove from the heat and add the chocolate. Let stand until the chocolate softens, about 2 minutes. Add the grappa. Whisk until the chocolate melts and the mixture is completely smooth. Pour into the cooled pastry shell. Refrigerate until the filling is cooled and set to a pudding-like consistency, about 1 hour.

3. Arrange the raspberries close to each other on top of the chocolate filling. Refrigerate until the filling is completely chilled, at least 1 hour and up to 1 day. Just before serving, sift confectioners' sugar over the raspberries. Serve chilled or at room temperature.

CRUNCHY ALMOND COOKIE-CAKE

Torta sbrisolona

● ●

Makes 6 to 8 servings

Sbriciolato *means crumbled, which is exactly the delectable texture of this big cookie that thinks it is cake. You do not need any serious baking skills to create this nutty treat, and it is made entirely by hand. Don't cut it into neat wedges—it should be served at the table, broken into rough pieces, and eaten without forks. You will need two kinds of almonds, both sliced (which are easier to chop) and whole (for the decoration).*

8 ounces (2 sticks) unsalted butter, cut into tablespoons, at room temperature, plus more for the pan
¾ cup plus 4 tablespoons sugar
1½ cups sliced almonds (blanched or natural), coarsely chopped
2 cups (280 grams) unbleached all-purpose flour

1 cup yellow cornmeal, preferably stone-ground
2 large egg yolks
Finely grated zest of 1 lemon
2 teaspoons vanilla extract or seeds from 1 vanilla bean
12 whole almonds (preferably natural, with skins), for decoration

1. Position a rack in the center of the oven and preheat the oven to 350°F. Lightly butter a 9-inch springform pan.

2. Add ¾ cup plus 2 tablespoons of the sugar, the chopped almonds, flour, cornmeal, butter, egg yolks, lemon zest, and vanilla extract to a large bowl. Using your fingertips, rub the ingredients together until they are uniformly mixed but still crumbly. A handful at a time, press the dough together in your fist, and then crumble it into the prepared pan. It should remain very rough looking. Press the whole almonds into the dough in a decorative pattern. Sprinkle with the remaining 2 tablespoons sugar.

3. Bake until the cake is golden brown and has shrunk slightly from the sides of the pan, about 45 minutes. Let the cake cool in the pan on a wire cake rack. Remove the sides of the pan and transfer the cake to a platter. Serve with a dinner knife, allowing each guest to cut off their portion, and eat with their hands.

CHOCOLATE HAZELNUT BROWNIES

Brownies al cioccolato e nocciole

•••

Makes 9 brownies

D: *Nutella is the chocolate and hazelnut spread that is on almost every Italian's short list of favorite indulgences. Gabriele is very happy to find it at our local market. It is typically spread on bread as an afternoon snack with a glass of milk. But there is no reason why it can't be used as an ingredient in desserts, as it is here for these fudgy, chewy brownies. And there's another great thing about this recipe— you can make the batter in a single pot and have it ready for the oven in about 15 minutes.*

2 ounces (½ stick) unsalted butter, plus more for the pan

⅔ cup (95 grams) unbleached all-purpose flour, plus more for dusting

2 tablespoons unsweetened cocoa powder, preferably Dutch-processed

¼ teaspoon sea salt

1 bar (3.5 ounces) bittersweet (about 70% cacao) chocolate, coarsely chopped

⅔ cup chocolate-hazelnut spread, such as Nutella

1 cup sugar

1 teaspoon vanilla extract

2 large eggs, at room temperature

½ cup toasted, skinned, and coarsely chopped hazelnuts (see Tip)

1. Position a rack in the center of the oven and preheat the oven to 350°F. Lightly butter an 8-inch square baking pan. Line the pan on the bottom and up two sides with a strip of parchment paper or nonstick aluminum foil. Dust the inside of the pan with flour and tap out the excess flour.

2. Whisk the flour, cocoa, and salt together in a small bowl. Melt the butter in a medium saucepan over medium-low heat. Remove from the heat and add the chocolate. Let stand for 3 minutes. Whisk until the chocolate melts. Add the chocolate-hazelnut spread and whisk until smooth, followed by the sugar and vanilla. One at a time, whisk in the eggs, waiting until each egg is absorbed before adding the next. Stir (do not whisk) in the flour mixture, followed by the hazelnuts. The batter will be thick. Spread evenly in the prepared pan.

3. Bake until a wooden toothpick inserted in the center of the pastry comes out with a moist crumb, 25 to 30 minutes. Let cool completely in the pan on a wire rack. Run a knife around the pan to loosen the pastry. Use the paper "handles" to lift the pastry out of the pan in one piece. Cut into 9 brownies. (The brownies can be wrapped in plastic wrap and stored at room temperature for up to 2 days.)

TIP To toast and skin hazelnuts, spread the hazelnuts in a rimmed baking sheet. Bake in a preheated 350°F oven, stirring occasionally, until the skins are cracked and the nuts look light brown underneath the skins, 10 to 15 minutes. Transfer the hazelnuts to a kitchen towel and let stand until cooled, about 20 minutes. Rub the nuts against each other in the towel to remove the skins. Don't worry if some of the skins are stubborn and don't come off. To "chop" the nuts, it is easiest to actually crush them on a carving board with a flat meat tenderizer or the bottom of a moka (Italian coffee) pot.

CHOCOLATE CHIP AND ESPRESSO COOKIES

Biscotti al cioccolato e caffè

• •

Makes about 3 dozen cookies

D: *Cookies are often an afterthought for Italian home bakers, with the holiday variety being an exception. When you go to a Tuscan bakery, you will see many luscious* tortas, *and some long, crisp biscotti, but certainly not cookies the size of your palm. Of course, in America, cookies are everywhere. When Gabriele encountered his first chocolate chip cookie, there was an immediate attraction, but he could not resist adding some ground coffee to balance its sweetness and add an Italian touch. Try this with your afternoon espresso or a cold glass of milk during a TV binge-watching session.*

2¼ cups (315 grams) unbleached all-purpose flour
½ teaspoon baking soda
1 tablespoon finely ground Italian- or French-roast coffee
¾ teaspoon sea salt

8 ounces (2 sticks) unsalted butter, at room temperature
1 cup packed light brown sugar
½ cup granulated sugar
1½ teaspoons vanilla extract
2 large eggs, at room temperature
2 cups (12 ounces) semisweet chocolate chips

1. Position racks in the top third and center of the oven and preheat the oven to 350°F. Line two large rimmed baking sheets with parchment paper or silicone baking mats.

2. Whisk the flour, baking soda, ground coffee, and salt together in a large bowl. Beat the butter in a large bowl with an electric mixer set on high speed until smooth. Gradually beat in the brown and granulated sugars and continue beating until the mixture is light in color and texture, about 3 minutes. Beat in the vanilla. One at a time, beat in the eggs. Reduce the mixer speed to low. Beat in the flour mixture. Stop the mixer and stir in the chocolate chips.

3. Using a rounded tablespoon for each cookie, drop the dough onto the baking sheets, spacing them about 2 inches apart. Bake, switching the positions of the sheets from top to bottom and front to back halfway through baking, until the edges are lightly browned, about 12 to 15 minutes. Do not overbake. Let the cookies cool on the sheets for 3 minutes. Transfer them to wire racks to cool completely. Repeat with the remaining dough on cooled baking sheets. (The cookies can be stored in an airtight container at room temperature for up to 3 days.)

MOM'S CHOCOLATE PUDDING

Budino della mamma al cioccolato

••••••••••••••••••••••••••••••

Makes 6 servings

G: *My goal here was to create an amped-up version of my mom's chocolate pudding. My brother, Fabio, and I were not the only kids who loved that dessert. Mamma used to buy boxes of imported German pudding, and she would make big batches to serve to my brother and me. As a grown-up, I wanted the same smooth texture, but maybe a hint of espresso to deepen the flavor . . . and here it is. I love the contrast of the tart lemon zest with the sweet chocolate, which is truly an "adults only" addition. One spoonful of this pudding, and I am transported back to afternoons on the sofa watching cartoons.*

BUDINO
½ cup granulated sugar
2 tablespoons cornstarch
1 tablespoon natural unsweetened cocoa
    powder
1 tablespoon coarsely ground Italian- or
    espresso-roast coffee
Pinch sea salt
2¾ cups whole milk
¼ cup heavy cream
4 large egg yolks
1 vanilla bean, split lengthwise, or 1 teaspoon
    vanilla extract

4 ounces semisweet chocolate (about 55%
    cacao), finely chopped
1 ounce bittersweet chocolate (about 70%
    cacao), finely chopped

WHIPPED CREAM
1 cup heavy whipping cream
2 tablespoons confectioners' sugar
1 teaspoon vanilla extract

1 lemon, for garnish

1. To make the *budino*: Whisk the sugar, cornstarch, cocoa powder, ground coffee, and salt together in a large saucepan. (It is important to combine the sugar, cornstarch, and cocoa well at this point because they thicken at different rates. If you just casually mix them together, the pudding will be lumpy.) Gradually whisk in the milk, followed by the heavy cream and egg yolks, and whisk until smooth. Using the tip of a small knife, scrape in the vanilla seeds from the bean into the milk mixture, and add the empty pod too. (Do not add the vanilla extract yet, if using.)

2. Whisk over medium heat, making sure that the pudding is not sticking to the bottom and corners of the saucepan, until the pudding comes to a full boil and thickens, 6 to 8 minutes. Remove from the heat. Add the semisweet and bittersweet chocolate and let stand until they soften, about 3 minutes. Whisk until the chocolates melt into the pudding.

3. Strain the pudding through a medium-mesh sieve into a medium bowl. Don't rub the pudding through the sieve with a spoon or spatula. Instead, rap the edge of the sieve against the rim of the bowl. Discard the vanilla pod. (If using vanilla extract, stir it in now.) Divide the pudding equally

among six 6-ounce ramekins or 8-ounce glass jars. Cover the top of each pudding with plastic wrap, pressing the wrap directly onto the surface to keep a skin from forming. Refrigerate until chilled and set, about 3 hours or overnight.

4. To make the whipped cream: Whip the cream, confectioners' sugar, and vanilla in a chilled large bowl with an electric hand mixer set at high speed until the mixture forms mounds that barely hold their shape.

5. Uncover each pudding and top with a dollop of whipped cream. Using a citrus zester (the kind that has 4 or 5 small holes) or a microplane, grate some of the lemon zest over each pudding, and serve chilled.

LIMONCELLO AND MASCARPONE PARFAITS

Crema di mascarpone e limoncello

•••

Makes 6 servings

A tart lemon dessert is always a refreshing way to end a meal, and these parfaits prove the point. Recipes for homemade limoncello abound online (and there's one in our first book), although store-bought versions work well too. Be sure not to let the cookies soak in the limoncello syrup—a quick dip is all they need.

LIMONCELLO SYRUP
¼ cup sugar
2 tablespoons limoncello

MOUSSE
3 large eggs, separated
4 tablespoons sugar
One 8-ounce container of mascarpone cheese,
    at room temperature
2 tablespoons limoncello

Zest of ½ lemon
9 Italian ladyfingers (*savoiardi*), each cut
    crosswise into quarters for 36 pieces total
6 ounces fresh blueberries or raspberries (about
    1⅓ cups)
6 sprigs fresh basil or mint (optional)

1. To make the syrup: Bring ⅓ cup water and the sugar to a boil in a small saucepan over high heat, stirring to dissolve the sugar. Boil for 1 minute. Remove from the heat and let cool completely. Stir in the limoncello.

2. To make the mousse: Beat the egg yolks and 2 tablespoons of the sugar together in a small bowl with a handheld electric mixer set on high speed (or a whisk) until the mixture is thick and pale yellow, about 1 minute (or 2 minutes for the whisk).

3. Using a rubber spatula, mash the mascarpone, limoncello, and lemon zest in a medium bowl until the cheese is smooth and free of lumps. Fold in the yolk mixture.

4. Using clean beaters (or a clean whisk), whip the egg whites and the remaining 2 tablespoons sugar together in a clean medium bowl just until soft, shiny peaks form. Stir in one-third of the whites into the mascarpone mixture to lighten it. Fold in the remaining whites.

5. Pour the cooled syrup into a shallow bowl. Place 6 wine glasses or glass dessert bowls on the work surface. For each parfait, quickly dip 3 ladyfinger quarters into the syrup, just to moisten them—do not soak. Spoon about ⅓ cup of the mousse into the glass and top with about 3 tablespoons of the berries. Repeat with the same amount of dipped ladyfingers, mousse, and berries. Discard any remaining syrup. Cover each glass and refrigerate for at least 1 hour or up to 8 hours.

6. To serve, top each glass with a sprig of basil, if using, and serve chilled.

BLOOD ORANGE STRACCIATELLA SEMIFREDDO

Semifreddo di arancia e cioccolato

....

Makes 6 to 8 servings

True, stracciatella is Italy's egg drop soup (page 57), but the term (which means "ragged" in Italian) also refers to gelato with chocolate flakes. (You don't find classic chocolate chips at the typical Italian supermarket.) Semifreddo is a crowd-pleasing frozen dessert that is especially useful because it doesn't require an ice-cream machine. As its name suggests, the texture is semi-frozen and creamy. While blood oranges give this a distinct Italian profile, you can use navel oranges. And, if you wish, garnish each serving with orange supremes (see step 1, page 71).

4 blood oranges
1 cup sugar
5 large eggs, at room temperature
2 tablespoons orange marmalade, preferably bitter orange

1 cup heavy cream
3 ounces bittersweet chocolate (about 70% cacao), finely chopped
Orange slices and fresh mint sprigs, for garnish

1. Finely grate the zest from 1½ oranges. Juice the 4 oranges; you need ¾ cup juice. Strain the juice.

2. Bring the blood orange juice to a boil in a small saucepan over medium heat. Cook until it reduces to ⅓ cup. (Use a measuring cup here, and don't estimate it. You want to reduce the amount of water in the juice so the *semifreddo* isn't icy and to increase the intensity of the orange flavor.) Stir in the sugar and cook until the mixture comes to a full boil—it will bubble up, so be careful.

3. Whip the eggs in a stand mixer with the whisk attachment on high speed until they triple in volume and are thick and pale yellow, about 3 minutes. During the last 30 seconds of whipping, return the orange syrup to a full boil over high heat. Transfer the syrup to a liquid measuring cup. With the mixer running, slowly pour the syrup into the eggs, being sure not to pour the syrup directly into the beater. Whip until the mixture is cool (feel the bottom of the bowl to check), about 6 minutes. Beat in the marmalade and orange zest.

4. Using a handheld electric mixer on high speed or a whisk, whip the cream in a large chilled bowl until stiff. Fold the whipped cream into the egg mixture.

5. Line a 9 by 5 by 3-inch loaf pan with a double thickness of plastic wrap, letting the excess plastic wrap hang over the sides. In thirds, spread the *semifreddo* mixture in the prepared pan, sprinkling each layer with one-third of the chocolate. Cover with the overhanging wrap. Freeze until the *semifreddo* is frozen, at least 6 hours or overnight. Freeze a serving platter at the same time.

6. To serve, fold back the overhanging plastic. Invert and unmold the *semifreddo* onto the chilled platter and discard the plastic. Garnish with the oranges and mint, cut into slices, and serve immediately.

CHOCOLATE "SALAME"

Salame al cioccolato

• •

Makes 6 to 8 servings

G: *Like all boys, I had more than one favorite dessert. But there was something about my family's chocolate salame that was fascinating because of its trompe l'oeil appearance—it looks just like a small salame coated with "bloom." (Try the tying-up with string, or skip it.) In Italy, we use the not-too-sweet, whole grain digestive cookies, actually a British import, for some of the filling. In the United States, I simply use graham crackers, which work very well. You can substitute other ingredients, such as pistachios or slivered almonds for some of the cookies.*

D: *This treat is a perfect sweet ending to a big meal—just enough to send everyone out happy, but not stuffed. It's one of my favorites, too, because it is so easy to make. In fact, our younger daughter, Giulia, is becoming quite an expert at making it.*

Special equipment: kitchen twine, for tying the salame (optional)

6 tablespoons (¾ stick) unsalted butter
12 ounces finely chopped bittersweet chocolate
   (about 70% cacao)
2 tablespoons honey

1 large egg, beaten (see Note, page 252)
1 cup coarsely broken (½-inch pieces) graham
   cracker cookies
2 tablespoons confectioners' sugar, as needed

1. Melt the butter in a medium saucepan over low heat. Remove from the heat and add the chocolate. Let stand until the chocolate is softened, about 3 minutes. Whisk until the chocolate is smooth and melted. Whisk in the egg and honey. Fold in the graham crackers.

2. Cover loosely with plastic wrap and refrigerate, taking out every 10 minutes or to scrape down the sides with a rubber spatula, until the mixture is cool and thickened, but not set, 30 minutes to 1 hour. (Watch closely, because the exact timing depends on the refrigerator temperature and the chocolate brand.)

3. Spread a 16-inch-long sheet of plastic wrap on a work surface. Spoon the chocolate mixture along the end of the plastic closest to you, forming a 12-inch log. Starting at the closest side, roll up the chocolate in the plastic to make a rough cylinder. Tightly twist the ends of the plastic in opposite directions to enclose and form the chocolate into a salame shape. Gently roll the salame on the work area to smooth the salame surface. Place it on a small baking sheet. Refrigerate until firm, at least 2 hours or overnight.

4. Unwrap the chocolate salame. Sift the confectioners' sugar all over the salame to coat it. Tie the kitchen twine, if using, around the salame crosswise at 1-inch intervals. (If you want a very authentic appearance, look online for directions on how to do a "butcher's knot" with a single long piece of kitchen twine.) The salame can be wrapped in plastic and refrigerated for up to 2 days.

5. To serve, let the salame stand at room temperature to soften slightly, about 15 minutes. Using a sharp knife, cut the salame into thin slices.

NOTE If you have concerns about using raw egg, use an organic egg or look for pasteurized eggs at well-stocked natural food stores and supermarkets.

ACKNOWLEDGMENTS

We would like to thank our families, on both sides of the ocean.

To the whole team at The Tuscan Gun, our small kitchen in Brooklyn: It is a great thing to have an extended family that can test and help develop new recipes with us. Thanks to you all!

To our neighborhood, for having welcomed and supported us, and for always keeping it real! Raising our children in this community has had a huge impact on our family. We belong here now, and that is a very powerful feeling.

Rick Rodgers, your ability to capture the essence of our kitchen and family life made this project fun and personal. Your theatrical acumen helped you understand our thespian family, and we already are missing our long days of writing and eating and talking about history and technique. Thank you so much, too, for your dry wit. It has been a blast.

Eric Wolfinger, since we met three years ago to work on our first book we knew we made a friend forever. We have been counting the days until we could again tell a story with your images, and here we are. Thank you so much for your artistry, your humbleness, understanding our vision, and above all, bringing it to life.

Food stylist Simon Andrews, we were amazed at your ability to combine elegance and simplicity in all the dishes you cooked during the shoot. You are definitely ready to move with us to Tuscany! Thank you for your talent, light touch, and dedication. It has been a joy to work with you—let's do it again soon!

To our prop stylist, Alma Espinola, photographer assistant Connor Bruce, and assistant food stylist Janine Desiderio: We are so proud and honored to have had the privilege of working together. The two weeks of photography were sure a hustle but fun each and every second. Thank you so very much for your incredible abilities and the hard work you have put into this project. We will be missing our scrumptious lunch breaks!

Cara Bedick, you have offered great guidance and support to this new book of ours. We are so very grateful for your many contributions to this work with each step we took together. Also on the book "nuts and bolts" side, we would like to thank our diligent copy editor, Cecilia Molinari, and production manager Sarah Wright. Erich Hobbing is responsible for the book's beautiful design. Also, we want to acknowledge the hard work of our publicists, Shida Carr and Carrie Bachman.

Many thanks go to our literary agent, David Vigliano, for introducing us to the wonderful team at Touchstone. Also to Michelle Howry, for believing in us from the very beginning of the project.

INDEX

Note: Page numbers in *italics* refer to illustrations.

ABOUT THE AUTHORS

Debi Mazar, a native New Yorker, made her film debut in Martin Scorsese's *Goodfellas* and has since appeared in more than seventy feature films, as well as HBO's hit series *Entourage* and TV Land's new series *Younger*.

Gabriele Corcos was raised in a Tuscan olive orchard, on the hills right above Florence. He started cooking at the age of six and has not stopped since. Together, he and Debi produced and cohosted the Cooking Channel's *Extra Virgin*. They live in Brooklyn with their two daughters where they own the restaurant The Tuscan Gun.

Rick Rodgers is an award-winning cookbook author and culinary teacher. He has written over fifty cookbooks, both on his own and as a coauthor with many chefs, celebrities, restaurants, and bakeries.